Patterns in the *Myst*

Messages from the Universe

(Volume II of the *Myst* Series)

by Drs. Alex and David Bennet

Volume I: Journey into the *Myst*
Volume II: Patterns in the *Myst*
Volume III: The Heart, the Mind and the *Myst*

MQIPress (2020)
Frost, West Virginia
ISBN 978-1-949829-30-3

The human experience is a neuronal dance with the Universe.

We have read both The Journey into the Myst *and this sequel expansion of that information into scientific observation and facts. Let me explain how we became involved, and why this book is so key to learning how the Myst forms. We met the Bennets just after they opened The Inn at Mountain Quest in the early 2000s, and they are the last scientific-minded couple anyone would expect to encounter non-random interaction with energy and embrace it as a connection to phenomena in which they interact regularly in the presence of many others.*

We first experienced the Myst when Alex asked if we were interested in shooting some photos of it. Although we were skeptical, within the first few shots of her camera, the two of us experienced seeing the Myst swirl around her camera, us, and the farmyard in the cold night air. Upon taking the camera card in and viewing the pictures on our laptop, we saw several formations which appeared to be people, animals, and angels with wings. Upon closer inspection when blowing up the images, we saw vapor drops forming into the Myst, and many small faces within the vapor! We then learned more of their adventure from both of the Bennets and read The Journey into the Myst *to learn the whole story of how the Myst phenomenon began.*

Once we heard Patterns in the Myst *was released, we read it immediately.* Patterns in the Myst *further defines the formations which have been observed, how they form and are created with non-randomness by a form of intelligent sources beyond our earthly comprehension. Many key formation patterns are identified and shown by excellent Myst example photos. This book shifts styles from* The Journey into the Myst, *where that approach to telling the story of the Myst was more fascination-styled. This book shows familiar patterns encountered, and elaborates on our understanding more about the Myst through scientific evaluation, knowledge comparison, and very well-documented photos as evidence. Our minds may tend to believe a wonderful tale through our love of storytelling, but this book answers our logical questions of whether the Myst is for real and a scientifically-documented truth.* Patterns in the Myst *has an abundance of answers to many questions on the Myst formation, and facts about the reality of its existence.*

– Jeff and Becky Morehead, Morehead Marketing & Photography

Original version of Parts I and II (as eBooks) 2013
First Printing soft cover 2020
Copyright © 2020 MQIPress. All rights reserved.

In the spirit of collaborative advantage, with attribution,
any part of this book may be copied and distributed freely.

MQIPress
Frost, West Virginia
303 Mountain Quest Lane
Marlinton, WV 24954
United States of America
Telephone: 304-799-7267

alex@mountainquestinstitute.com
www.mountainquestinstitute.com
www.mountainquestinn.com
www.MQIPress.com
www.Myst-art.com

ISBN 978-1-949829-30-3

Nestled between Earth and Sky, Day and Night,

Lies a mystical realm where past and present meet the future.

For each of us there is a Gate to open, a Threshold to cross,

Where timeless truths remind us, we are not alone.

Volume II

Table of Contents

Table of Contents | i

Preface | iii

Chapter 1: Introduction to Patterns | 1
    Shapes as Patterns | 3
    Borders | 6

Chapter 2: Non-Random Patterns | 7
    Randomness in Terms of Picture Color | 7
    Environmental Impact | 9
    Repeated Patterns | 10
    Non-Randomness in Terms of Response | 10

Chapter 3: Pattern Recognition in Terms of Textures | 12
    Circles | 12
    Pocked | 14
    Clouds | 14
    Fluff | 17
    Dots | 18
    Squirms | 20
    Soft Light and Bright Light |
    In Summary | 25

Chapter 4: Patterns of Response | 27
    External and Internal Conditions | 27
    Resonance | 28
    The Power of Intention | 29
    Interacting with the *Myst* | 31
    An Evening of Play | 32

Chapter 5: Patterns Across the *Myst* | 36
    Elemental Energy | 37
    Faces | 40
    Guide Clouds | 44
    Riders of the *Myst* | 46

Chapter 6: Interpretation and Meaning | 48
    Meaning | 49
    Meaning Unfolding | 52
    Animals | 54
    Juxtaposing Positive and Negative Energies | 58

Chapter 7: Taking a Closer Look | 62
    What does God Look Like? | 62
    Child of the Universe | 64
    Cloaked Visitors | 65
    Music and Rhythm in the *Myst* | 67
    Crowned with Light | 69

Chapter 8: A Stream of Angels | 71
    Myst Angels Wrapped in Pinks | 74

Chapter 9: The Physics of the *Myst* | 77
1. Water Molecules are used to form the *Myst* | 77
2. Orbs are integral to forming the *Myst* | 79
3. The *Myst* is affected by weather conditions | 80
4. The *Myst* presents with a variety of energetic properties | 82
5. The Myst appears through a "coupling" of molecular physical reality and magnetic resonance physical reality (Tiller) | 84

Chapter 10: Messages in the *Myst* | 85

Endnotes | 90

Appendix A: Textures of the Myst | 93

References | 95

Index | 97

About Mountain Quest | 99

Preface

For a number of days now, I've been trying to think of something profound to say in this Preface. Only I keep coming back to the realization that this is me, just me, writing, and I feel so humble to have had and continue to have the amazing experience of the *Myst*.

This experience is detailed in the first book in the series, *The Journey into the Myst*. It begins with a miracle, which no doubt was necessary to open our hearts and minds to what was coming. When the physical healing from this initial experience was well along, exposure to the energy and light of the Universe began, such that the wonderful connections of which we all are a part have moved into conscious awareness, with joy bubbling up within experience after experience. Even my partner, who throughout life has been proud to call himself a scientist and skeptic, was pulled into this energy and, ever so slowly—through repeated experiences, research and tests—began to unfold a new understanding of our larger connections. The two of us now agree, from the limited framework of being human, that physics is metaphysics made known.

Something profound, worthy of the *Myst* experience? These are certainly profound times we are living through, and I wonder if the *Myst* was a gift to help prepare us for these times? Understanding that we are a part of this larger field—whether we choose to call it an energy field, consciousness field, Quantum field, or God field—certainly enables us to look at life from an expanded perspective.

The secluded beauty of the 2020 lockdown, especially at this writing when the phone service has been off for several days, has offered the opportunity for considerable self-reflection, as well as the time to accomplish so many things that I've promised myself to do while still present in this life. For example, finally making the *Myst* series available in a soft cover format, so readers can truly enjoy the beauty of the *Myst*, and finally writing the third book in the series, *The Heart, the Mind and the Myst*. That is now underway, with several wonderful co-authors.

This second book in the series, *Patterns in the Myst*, has a primarily mental focus based on the belief that nothing is purely random, and, if we look closely enough, there are messages in the *Myst*, that is, learning to be had. And, sure enough, messages have continued to pour through since those initial experiences nearly ten years ago. One of the ways we've shared those messages is through a series of little Conscious Look Books titled *Possibilities that are YOU!* Each of these little books, conversational in nature, offers seven ideas around topics unfolding for the veteran of life experience. These are things we are all learning brought into consciousness; things such as balance, intuition, grounding, thought adjusting, beauty, truth, creativity, compassion, and so many more topics that help us fully become the co-creators of our reality.

As you explore the pictures and observations reflected in this second book in the series, perhaps it is *your* thoughts and feelings which will move us towards profoundness. We are pleased to share this book with you in this new format, with added pictures, as together we journey further into the *Myst*.

Love and Light,
Alex and David

The Drs. Alex and David Bennet live at the Mountain Quest Institute, Inn and Retreat Center situated on a 430-acre farm in the Allegheny Mountains of West Virginia. See www.mountainquestinn.com and www.mountainquestinstitute.com For information or reservations for the Inn, call 304-799-7267. Alex may be contacted at alex@mountainquestinstitute.com

Chapter 1: Introduction to Patterns

What are patterns really? The term "pattern" comes from the French word *patron* which is a specific theme that reoccurs in events, objects, or movement. Patterns can be based on repetition (the same thing appearing again and again) and periodicity (recurrence at regular intervals), similarity (likeness, qualities or features in common), or symmetry (balanced proportions, exact correspondence in position) and translation (a change in form or state, transference to a different place).

Patterns are one of two foundational concepts of the Universe. The other is energy. Thus, from the most basic perspective of physics, the Universe is made up of patterns of energy—nothing more, nothing less. If a specific pattern is not random, then it contains information. This is why some physicists consider energy and information to be the basic properties of the Universe.[1]

Whether a specific non-random pattern is recognized as information depends on the individual looking at the pattern. For example, if the pattern is a Chinese symbol and the observer does not understand Chinese and is not capable of interpreting the pattern of the symbol, then the observer acquires no information from the symbol. However, to a Chinese observer the same symbol may contain huge meaning.

Building on this idea, any given pattern may contain different information for different observers. Many people have different interpretations, that is, they get different information from the same pattern. These differences happen for a number of reasons. First, we tend to see what we are looking for, what we are interested in, or what strikes an emotional chord in us. Since no two people are alike (different DNA, beliefs, passions, etc.), the things we are looking for, interested in, or emotionally charged about can be quite different. A reader may find personal connections happening frequently while looking at the *Myst-Art* photographs in this book! Second, the interpretation and meaning of incoming patterns are very much a function of preexisting patterns in the brain. Each individual has had different experiences in life (culture, family, activities, work, etc.), all of which are reflected in the patterns in the individual's brain.

Interpreting patterns is one of the main functions of the brain—it is how we learn. David Kolb (1984), a professor and well-known expert on Experiential Learning, proposes four ways in which we learn. One is by concrete experience, the second is by reflective observation, the third is by abstract conceptualization, and the fourth is by active experimentation. When we have **direct experience** (such as observing and feeling) and become aware of our reaction to what we are observing we are learning through Apprehension. We are listening to our body, our intuition and our overall reaction through the senses. When we consciously **reflect on what we are observing**, perhaps pulling up our past experiences that relate to what we see, and then cognitively think about it, we are using our Comprehension to learn and understand. Both approaches are viable and can aid in learning and interpreting events, situations and/or patterns. Sometimes our unconscious (emotions and feelings) may give us a better understanding of a phenomenon than our conscious mind (logical and analytical). Both are applicable and useful in interpreting the complex patterns within the *Myst* photographs.

People are ALWAYS looking for relationships among things—events, happenings, people, thoughts. Our brains work as associative patterners, that is, everything that comes in through all of the senses and everything that is stored in millions and billions of patterns within the mind/brain and body is continuously being mixed, matched and complexed.[2] This process of associative patterning is the process of continuously creating new patterns which *have the potential* to lead to information and perhaps knowledge in our continuous quest for understanding and meaning. The very important difference between information and knowledge is addressed in Chapter 6.

Much like patterns in nature, the *Myst* is somewhat chaotic, never *exactly* repeating a pattern, though there may be consistency in a number of similar elements. In addition to looking for those things which repeat themselves (characteristics, appearance, response, etc.), the authors have attempted to develop some *common principles* behind similar patterns of *Myst*. For example, Mountain Quest Institute's Quarter Horse Paint mare named Vision Quest is brown and white. While her mother (Calamity Jane) had different markings or patterns, nonetheless they are both Quarter Horse Paint mares that are brown and white. These are high-level similarities, although digging deeper into personality characteristics or the pattern of their brown and white markings would also provide similarities as well as differences. Given a set of similar characteristics, the question then becomes whether this set applies to all/most Quarter Horse Paint mares that are brown and white?

Pattern formation in developmental biology is the mechanism by which equivalent cells assume complex forms and functions. In science pattern formation is the visible and ordered outcomes of self-organization built on a set of common principles. We ask: Are there underlying common principles behind the *Myst* phenomena? How deep can we delve to help identify differences, discover similarities and uncover meaning? Meaning, of course, is often our most desirable goal. Specifically, how can we interpret the patterns to glean meaning, or how does the pattern impact our thoughts, lives, actions or beliefs?

 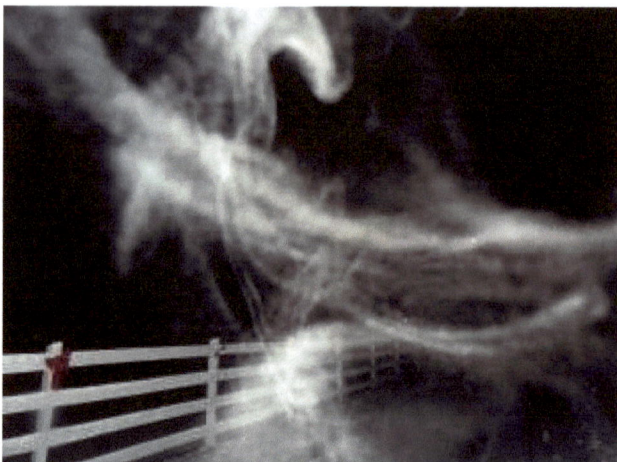

What comes to mind when we observe these patterns?

Patterns often provide information. By studying them carefully we may gain insights and understanding of what information they represent. One approach to pattern recognition is the assignment of labels to a given input. For example, developing a classification or clustering system such as that which we present when discussing the textures of the *Myst*. Over time observation of these textures (attributes) gently leads us to think of specific characteristics in terms of energy output, which in turn leads us to explore potential sources of those energy outputs. Another approach to pattern recognition is exploring the probability of a specific characteristic occurring. The probability of a *Myst* pattern occurring is introduced in Chapter 2 using the characteristic of color.

Each of us may see *different* patterns in a picture … and this is good! Patterns can generate new ideas through our emotions and intellect, and perhaps relate to things we have experienced recently in our lives.

This element of pattern recognition—as well as a meaning-making approach called Dihedral Group Theory developed by Dr. Tom McCabe[3]—will be explored in Chapter 6 on interpretation and meaning. But before moving into these specific areas, let's take a look at various patterns that occur throughout the *Myst* phenomena.

SHAPES AS PATTERNS

Shapes (form) are patterns that bound space. In our four-dimensional world, shapes immediately convey the three spatial dimensions of height, width and breadth. From this perspective, the fourth dimension is, of course, time. One of the early questions regarding the *Myst* was whether it was two dimensional or three dimensional. Because it is only seen when the flash is used, it is generally seen from a viewpoint that is two dimensional. To explore this question Alex began using two cameras, two flashes, coming from different directions. David and Alex would also stand at right angles and work to synchronize their pictures. In this way, they were able to capture a specific picture from two different angles. Upon repeating this process, it became increasingly clear that the *Myst* was presenting itself as (at a minimum) three dimensional patterns.

It is significant—and perhaps expected—that orbs take the shape of a sphere. The omnipresent sphere is a universally abundant shape, the shape from which all living things emerge and the beginning point of complex individuals (Volk, 1995).

Orbs frolic in the rock garden.

Examples of spheres in nature range from human ovaries to eggs; the fertilized eggs of frogs, sea urchins and worms to the green balls in freshwater algae colonies in various kinds of marine plankton; pulsars to black holes; and moons to planets and suns. Even atoms were originally thought of in terms of space-filling balls. As Volk describes:

When alone in space, like a miniature star, a hydrogen atom's cloud of charge density created by its single electron extends and fades into spherical infinity (the so-called 1s electron: s for spherical) ... The sphere thus appears to reign as dominant shape in the astronomically immense, the atomic infinitesimal, and the ancient or nascent living. No other shape is so universally abundant, so insistent as the omnipresent sphere. (Volk, 1995, p. 6)

There are many reasons why the sphere emerges as the prominent shape throughout nature. Energy is always conserved; you cannot create it or destroy it; you can only change its form and/or move it around. A compacted spherical surface area has significant biological advantages, providing the smallest surface and strongest structure for the greatest volume. Because it is a low maintenance shape, many cells are spherical. For example, the majority of cells in the human immune system (T-cells, B-cells, and the natural killer cells) are spherical.

In space, a liquid ball develops a "skin" that is self-created from surface tension. A leaky faucet demonstrates this same behavior as the water forms into a drop, naturally forming a skin as the fluids drive to achieve "states of lowest energy, which translates into the lowest total area of free surface" (Volk, 1995, p. 12).

When moving, spheres are omnidirectional, that is, when propelled **they can spin in any direction with minimal air resistance**. This would appear necessary and desirable for orbs. The importance of being omnidirectional can be seen in the use of balls in various sports and in early satellites, where their "roundness minimized drag with the upper reaches of the atmosphere, and they could tumble without orientation whilst sending beeps to Earth" (Volk, 1995, p. 10).

The sphere shape has been recognized throughout history as reflecting power. For example, spheres are often depicted in the hand of Jesus; a sphere is the jewel for wish-granting in the hand of the Buddhist bodhisattva; the sphere is the Orb of power held by European kings and queens; and the sphere appears under the paws of sculpted lions such as the Florentine lion in the Piazza della Signoria.

Thus, physical attributes of spheres such as omnidirectionality, surface area and strength are part of the sphere's archetypal attributes equating power, equanimity, idealization, and perfection (Volk, 1995, p. 22). These connections are observed in *Timaeus*, where Plato describes the origins of the universe.

Creator compounded the world ... as far as possible a perfect whole and of perfect parts ... leaving no remnants out of which another such world might be created ... that figure ... which comprehends within itself all other figures ... the form of a globe, round as from a lathe, having its extremes in every direction equidistant from the center, the most perfect and the most like itself of all figures ... the surface smooth all around ... because the living being had no need of eyes when there was nothing remaining outside to be seen. (Hutchins, 1952)

Counterparts to the sphere are **sheets** (flat planes, similar to a pancake) and tubes (rounded lines, similar to a spaghetti noodle). In the biological world an example of sheets are the green leaves on plants used to absorb light, with a surface area enhancement that is 20-40 times greater than volume (Volk, 1995, p. 31). Another function of sheets related to energy transfer occurrences is the ability to capture motion. Examples are the ear drum (capturing sound waves) and the sail of a sailboat (capturing wind currents). Sheets also transfer matter, as occurs in the leaf as it gathers carbon dioxide, disposes of oxygen, and transpires water to cool the leaf (similar to human sweating). Energy and matter also carry messages through light, the universal bearer of differences that make a difference (Bateson, 1979). Sheets are different than spheres in their surface-to-volume ratios as well as in their directionality. For example, tossing a Frisbee is very different than throwing a baseball. Given the general viewpoint of two-dimensions in pictures, it is difficult to identify sheets in the *Myst* phenomenon, although it is assumed that they are present.

Like sheets, **tubes** have a greater surface area than spheres with equivalent volumes. In nature they too are used as transfer surfaces. For example, a pine needle captures photons and exchanges gases much more efficiently than if its biomass were shaped as a ball. Also, like sheets, tubes change momentum with their environment. However, they are not interchangeable in places that need surface because of their unique shapes. Examples include a kite (sheet) attached to a string (tube), and a canoe (sheet) guided by an oar (tube attached to a sheet). As Volk states, "Where the press of maximizing area overwhelmingly drives the design, sheets will dominate" (Volk, 1995, p. 34). A third major attribute of tubes is the ability to transfer forces along lines. Because they will encounter some degree of resistance, all forward-moving tubes in life and technology need a measure of rigidity as structural columns, to transfer the forces encountered from the front toward the back. This ability to transfer forces along lines is a third major function of tubes, and, for many, as structural tubes, their raison d'être. (Volk, 1995, p. 35).

Biological structural tubes are about reach. "The most efficient use of materials in support systems that reach out occurs in cylindrical bodies" (Wainwright, 1988, p. 17). As connectors, tubes are directional. They can also be thought of in terms of relationships between objects in space.

There are multiple examples of tubes in the *Myst*. One excellent example is a photograph titled "Entanglement" in the *Myst*-Art Gallery. These tube-like structures appear to be in relationship at their base with the larger *Myst* energy and to host faces at their extremes.

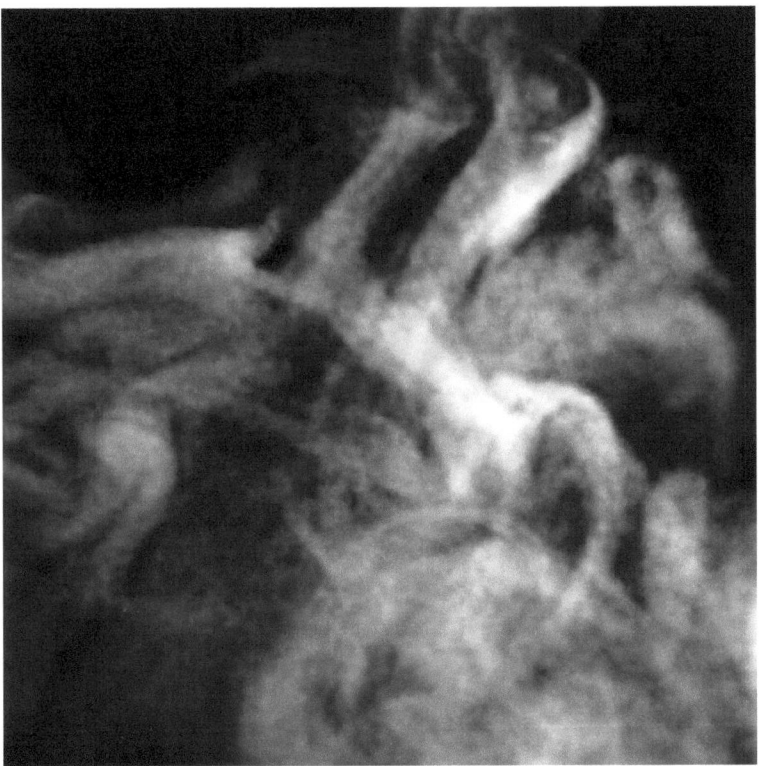

This picture titled "Entanglement" in the Myst-Art Gallery is described as:
"Bringing Myst-ical perspectives to the human mind by changing the way we view the world."

BORDERS

The surfaces of spheres, tubes and sheets can also be considered as borders which function as barriers to disruption. Distinct bounding surfaces can be found in all scales of life. For example, the generic design in biology's border is first to repel the drive toward disorder and, second, via repetition to facilitate growth. These surfaces provide a system of walls and bridges that serve both to separate and connect. The closest example to the *Myst* pictures would be the patterns in clouds. While clouds lack a defining skin (such as the boundaries of the human body), they sometimes terminate against the blue sky thus showing edges, and sometimes are fuzzy and indistinct, even wispy in nature (similar to the *Myst*). While these borders are casual, clouds are still recognized as things that are distinct, worthy of notice, and therefore named.

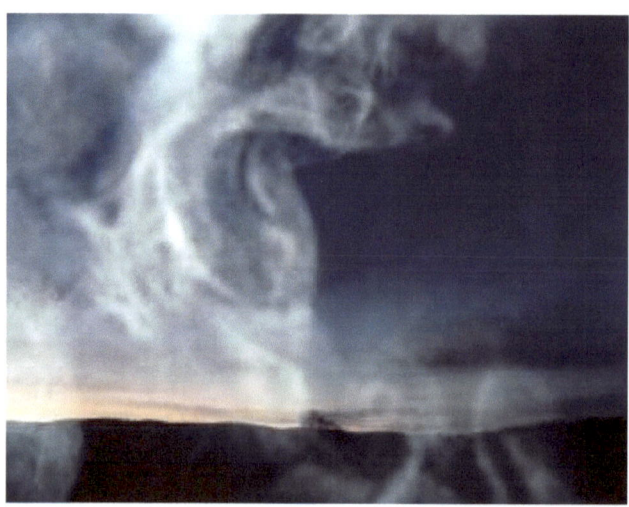

The complex, often shifting nature of the borders of clouds described above (moving in scale from large to small) is an example of fractal geometry. In the classical Euclidean geometry objects exist in integer dimensions, that is, single dimensional points, one dimensional lines and curves, two-dimensional plane figures (like circles and squares), and three-dimensional solid objects (like spheres and cubes). Depending on the amount of space it takes up as it twists and curves, a fractal curve in nature will have a dimension between one and two; a fractal landscape will have a dimension between two and three. (Volk, 1995, p. 57)

Similar to clouds, the shifting nature of the borders of the *Myst* may provide an example of fractal geometry. Some of the *Myst* photographs demonstrate two properties: (1) When part of the image is magnified it is essentially indistinguishable from the unmagnified version (self-similarity, or invariance under a change of scale) and, (2) some parts are irregular fragments. In nature the patterns that are the most highly symmetrical are often the most random. While they are not always visible, there are always differences at some level.

When Alex first began to see the *Myst* and capture it in her camera, because of the size and closeness of the *Myst* the pictures represented explosions of various textured light with no boundaries. She literally had a conversation with the *Myst*, saying that if this display was for her personally, she was convinced, but if she was to have pictures to study and share, the *Myst* had to present smaller shapes and forms (with boundaries) so that she could capture the entire pattern. We now have somewhere in the neighborhood of 47,000 pictures of the *Myst* available (we stopped counting at that number) to explore patterns. The real challenge and excitement come from extracting meaningful patterns and perhaps messages that lay within those patterns. Alex and David both believe that there are some pictures that are not random and therefore some intelligence that is creating the patterns. Why they believe this will unfold as you move through this book.

Recall that earlier we noted that all non-random patterns represent information. The American Heritage Dictionary (2006, p. 899) considers information to be a collection of facts or data or the condition of being informed. Thus, non-random patterns have the capacity to inform an observer. For this to happen there must be someone or something that has created the information. While we could speculate on their source here, let us save that for a later chapter. There are many phenomena that we do not understand; perhaps that is why the journey of life is so exciting.

Chapter 2: Non-Randomness as Probability

Probability is one way of helping to validate whether an event is based on an independent source. For purposes of this work, probability is considered the quality or condition of being probable or the likelihood that a given event will occur. This is often expressed as the ratio of the number of actual occurrences to the number of possible occurrences. Randomness is having no specific pattern, purpose or objective; relating to an event in which all outcomes are equally likely to occur. Non-randomness, then, means that the pattern, action or event may be anticipated from past and present patterns, actions or events, if (and only if) one has understood the patterns over time (sequences) well enough to predict the next pattern action or event.

There is a difference between non-randomness, predictability and uncertainty. Predictability means that one can successfully anticipate the probability of the next event, action or occurrence. Uncertainty means that one cannot successfully anticipate the next event, action or occurrence.

If the patterns in the *Myst* are random, then most likely they would be the result of the weather or other environmental conditions. If the patterns in the *Myst* are non-random, then **there is some influence or force—perceived or felt, internal or external, understood and/or beyond understanding—that is forming and shaping the patterns.** So, a first step in understanding the *Myst* and exploring the patterns in the *Myst* is understanding the probability that at least some of the *Myst* pictures contain some non-random parts. Each picture must contain either random or non-random parts, or some of both. By both we mean that part of the picture may be non-random (for example, the picture of the white fence in front of Mountain Quest) and another part of the pictures may be random (for example, an undefined *Myst* shape). There are also *Myst* patterns in some pictures that are clearly non-random which will be addressed later in the book.

RANDOMNESS IN TERMS OF PICTURE COLOR

Since this phenomenon began at Mountain Quest Institute in 2010, the pictures in the Gallery have been shot with either a 14.1, 16.1 or 18.2-megapixel camera. While other brands of cameras have been used for purposes of research, the photographer prefers using the Sony Cybershot, so the large majority of Gallery photographs were produced from this specific brand of camera. For purposes of this exploration into randomness in terms of color, we will assume a 14.1-megapixel camera.

While there may be more shades of colors involved in some of the photographs, for simplicity we consider three primary color tones: white, black and pink. By definition, if each pixel color is random then the probability of selecting any one of these colors at each pixel is the same for each color, that is, one out of three (1/3). This is the same as throwing dice. If there is a different number of dots on each side of a die (1, 2, 3, 4, 5 or 6) and if the die is balanced, the result should be random. The concept is similar with a perfectly balanced coin. In a random coin toss, the odds of tails versus heads should be the same, that is, both heads and tails have the same chance of being on top. Thus, for each coin toss the probability of the coin landing heads up is ½ and the probability of the coin landing tails up is also ½. This would be the probability for each coin toss.

With our three *Myst* colors, excluding external stimuli, it should be equally probable for any one color to appear in each pixel, that is, the probability of getting a black pixel is 1/3; the probability of getting a pink pixel is 1/3; and the probability of getting a white pixel is 1/3. So, in an unweighted environment with no external influences the probability of each pixel being a specific color is 1/3. In short, if each pixel of the camera's image were random then the pictures would be nothing more than a messy, complex mixture of black, white and pink dots.

If we look at a *specific order* of a string of pixels of the same color, the probability changes. For example, the probability of getting three black pixels in a row is 1/3 x 1/3 x 1/3 which is 1/27 or about 3.7%. As you can see, the probability is becoming very low. Suppose there are a hundred dots in a row? The probability is then $1/3^{100}$ which is equal to 1.94 x 10^{-48} (that's .194 with 47 zeros in front of it). This is a very, very low number, yet it is the probability of getting 100 black dots or 100 pink dots or 100 white dots in a row given no external influences.

Referring back to the picture frame and assuming an area of 100 pixels square (based on the width and height of the camera frame), there are 10,000 dots in the picture frame. When we do the calculations, if the color of each pixel is random **the probability of getting a picture in that area with a specific pattern** is infinitesimally small, but is not zero.

In the Myst pictures there may be many areas which are non-random due to trees, leaves, fences, etc. But we are interested in the areas of *Myst* in the pictures. Are the *Myst* shapes random patterns, or non-random patterns that may tell us something? If a pattern is non-random then it contains information and we may be able to interpret that information and learn and understand the meaning of the pattern.

To help understand this issue of randomness versus non-randomness, let's consider a *Myst* picture that will be the subject of meaning and interpretation later in this book.

In this photograph titled "The Gift of Light", given no external influence and an approximate 100 x 100-pixel square, the probability of the pink shape that appears in the photograph is about 3 x 10^{-96}.

As the sun was setting, this *Myst* picture was taken following the voicing of a specific question (discussed in Chapter 7 of this book). While the large swirling *Myst* in the right of the picture might be viewed as a face, it is the pink form in the lower left of the picture that is our example for purposes of considering probability. This pink shape could be viewed as the rough, but clearly bounded, molding of a human face. What creates those clear boundaries is the color pink, which is unique to the rest of the picture. The pink shape becomes even more prominent because of the splash of bright white behind it to the right. Similarly, there is the appearance of a light blue section of *Myst* shapes to the far bottom left. Putting aside (for now) the interpretation of the shapes themselves, the probability of this block of pink randomly appearing in the *Myst* picture without some external influence is extremely low.

Environmental Impact

Note that over and over again in the above explanation it has been specifically expressed as a given that no environmental effects were taken into consideration. In the reality in which photographs are taken there are ALWAYS environmental effects, some *reducing* the probability of randomness in a specific picture, and some *increasing* the probability of randomness in a specific picture.

An excellent example is other light sources. Moonlight (particularly a full moon) reflecting off a white source often creates a projection of the color blue. Thus, the camera might pick up a shade of blue for the area that was influenced by this light reflection. This would also influence the shape of the blue group of pixels, and might even influence visible shadows in the blue groups of pixels based on the surface evenness of the object being photographed that is reflecting the moonlight. However, when this does occur, the entire picture of the *Myst* reflects this blue tint, not a bounded part of the picture.

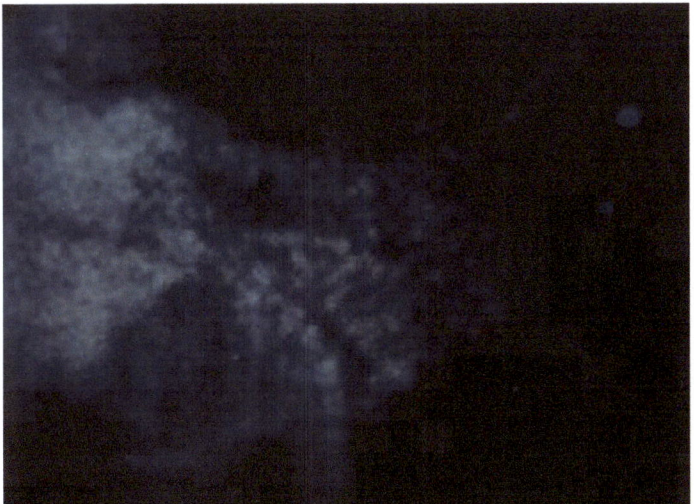 

(Left) When there is a full moon, the camera flash often picks up a shade of blue in the Myst picture. This is highly dependent on the direction of the picture, and when it does occur, the entire picture is affected. (Right) In contrast, here is a Myst picture where only the lower Myst shapes offer a blue tint, with different colors of pink juxtaposed to the blue.

The probabilities of impact from recognized environmental forces can be determined. For example, the probability of the impact on *Myst* pictures of wind currents is close to 100%. From looking at Alex's journal notes on weather conditions over a two-year period, it is apparent that the *Myst* does not appear during wind conditions. She has sometimes, however, been able to photograph orbs in wind conditions, with a large number of these pictures showing orbs in trees.

REPEATED PATTERNS

As we move through this book there will be a focus on repeated patterns, that is, shapes and forms that appear and reappear in multiple pictures captured at different times and places, thus increasing the probability of non-randomness. As introduced in the short discussion above, in probability location DOES matter. To create a specific form/shape and the characteristics we perceive from that form/shape (and continuing the example of three specific shades of colors), in two pixels next to each other there are nine different possibilities of order (B=Black, W=White, and P=pink): B-B, B-W, B-P; W-B, W-W, W-P; and P-B, P-W, P-P.

Thus, the non-random probability of a specific relationship or *ordering* among colors and shapes becomes even higher.

As an example, when you look at a large number of pictures you will find many faces, often first spotting two eyes (black dots) and then seeing the outline of the head or hair. Now ask yourself this question: If the patterns are random, why don't I see round, face-shaped areas with one, three or four black dots? You may think that you have seen these black dots but did not stop to look closely because they were not related to faces. Taking the time to relook at all of the pictures, you will rarely find one, three or four black dots. Why aren't they there if these pictures are random? While both authors agree that there are probably random patterns in some pictures, many of them are highly likely to be non-random.

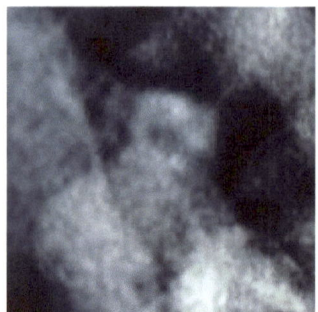 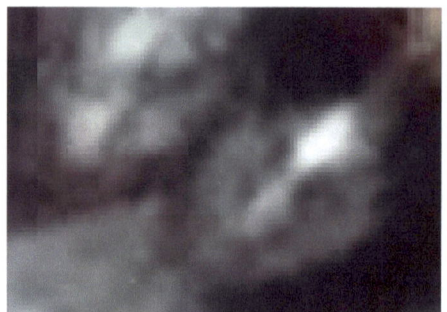 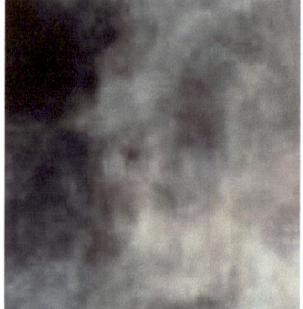 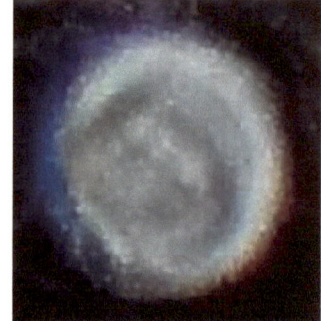

Faces emerge throughout the Myst.

In this discussion it is necessary to remember that nothing physical other than background items is in the picture prior to the flash exciting the *Myst* energies (see Chapter 9 for a discussion of the interaction between the flash and the orbs and *Myst*).

NON-RANDOMNESS IN TERMS OF RESPONSE

In the first book of the Mountain Quest Institute *Myst* Series (*The Journey into the Myst*, available as an eBook from Amazon) Alex worked out a system to ask "yes/no" questions when she was receiving a continuous stream of *Myst*. She asked the *Myst* (or the intelligence behind the forming of the *Myst*) to come directly in front of her camera if the answer to a question she asked was YES; and to move away and not appear in her camera if the answer was NO. She would repeat this process three times for each question to ensure that the response she was getting was non-random. Further, following three answers that were the same (in the picture for YES, not in the picture for NO), Alex would validate the answer by asking the *Myst* to do the opposite of the answer, that is, if the answer to the question was YES (*Myst* in the picture), she would ask the *Myst* to GO AWAY for her next shot (number 4), and then COME BACK into her picture on shot number 5. Thus, **it took five pictures to ensure that each answer was correct and validated as a potential non-random pattern**.

There were some environmental conditions necessary to ensure the validity of this response. Primarily, Alex had to ensure that the *Myst* had the potential to appear in every picture. Thus, this process of Q&A could only occur when she was receiving a continuous stream of *Myst,* that is, *Myst* appearing in her sight with every flash. Thus, the questioning would not begin until she felt sure that she was in a flow state with the *Myst*. A drawback here was the ability to remember the questions. When Alex achieved this continuous state of interaction with the *Myst,* she was in such a state of joy that the questions (and answers) didn't seem all that important, and the rigor of the process felt cumbersome.

One difficulty in validating the responses AFTER the session was that while the *Myst* might be seen by Alex through her eyes, it was not always situated exactly in front of the camera such that the camera lens picked it up. *Myst* could appear in the area of sky lit up by the flash without being in the area picked up by the camera lens. Nonetheless, Alex did record the questions and answers that she received in her journal. Many of these questions and responses were shared in the first eBook in this series.

Even more exciting to Alex were the personal picture responses to her questions. For example, when she asked if Mother Teresa was an angel an angel appeared in front of her, an appearance which was partially captured in her picture. While this experience was recorded by Alex and the picture is available as external validation, this occurrence was not externally observed, nor was it repeated. What gives strong support to the probability of non-randomness is the large number of picture responses provided in answer to questions by Alex.

Chapter 3: Pattern Recognition in Terms of Textures

One set of patterns discernible in the *Myst* is the perception of similar textures in the various pictures. While there is some level of judgment involved and the setting of limits when developing a model (and recognizing that any model is an artificial construct), models (names, categories, relationships, etc.) can help us understand the larger phenomenon of the *Myst*.

In the 47,000 or so[4] *Myst* photographs taken at Mountain Quest, there are patterns of textures that emerge over and over again. While many pictures display just one texture of the *Myst*, some pictures portray a variety of *Myst* textures. This diversity in itself increases the probability of non-randomness of the picture.

The specific physical make-up of the *Myst*—along with its boundary patterns, colored areas and density changes—seemingly imply (but do not prove) that there is some order and organization going on. As Stonier (1997) notes, "Information has, as one of its fundamental attributes, the capacity to organize things" (p. 19).

Another point that Stonier makes is that "a system may be said to contain information if such a system exhibits organization." (Stonier, 1997, p. 14). Many of the *Myst* pictures that Alex takes are composed of patterns that clearly indicate organization. Two that come immediately to mind are "The Gift of Light" introduced in Chapter 2 and "Friends of Light" introduced later in this chapter. Both pictures (and many others) contain patterns that could easily be understood by Alex and David as information. Note that a purely random picture, or pattern, would contain no organization or information.

Textures of the *Myst* pictures will be discussed in terms of: Circles, Pocked, Clouds, Fluff, Dots, Squirms, Soft Light and Bright Light. Charts showing "Textures of the *Myst*" are Appendix A.

CIRCLES

Perhaps the largest group of photographs appear to be made up of circles of light, strongly reflecting the idea of Orb origins (see Chapter 4). Using simple descriptive terms for ease of recall, this grouping is called **Circles**. Circles appeared in the *Myst* photograph of a Llama captured on October 2010, the photograph that began *The Journey into the Myst*. Despite the focus on textures, it is not surprising that the circle is the first descriptive term used in this chapter. Recall from Chapter 1 where we noted the significance of orbs taking the shape of a sphere, since the omnipresent sphere is a universally abundant shape, the shape from which all living things emerge and the beginning point of complex individuals (Volk, 1995). As its foundation, the *Myst* presents in circles.

In the example of Circles displayed in the photograph at the top of the next page (left), there is the appearance of "wings" which are comprised of circles of light. If we look closely and let our imagine play, there appear to be faces in many of the circles. This possibility is addressed later in this book.

In the descriptive category of Circles there are several anomalies that come into play. One of these is a crystalline look to the texture, often accompanied by a blue tint, which could potentially be explained by the presence of bright moonlight. In the example below, a special photograph offered during the Christmas season entitled "the Messenger", the blue tint contributes to the crystalline effect.

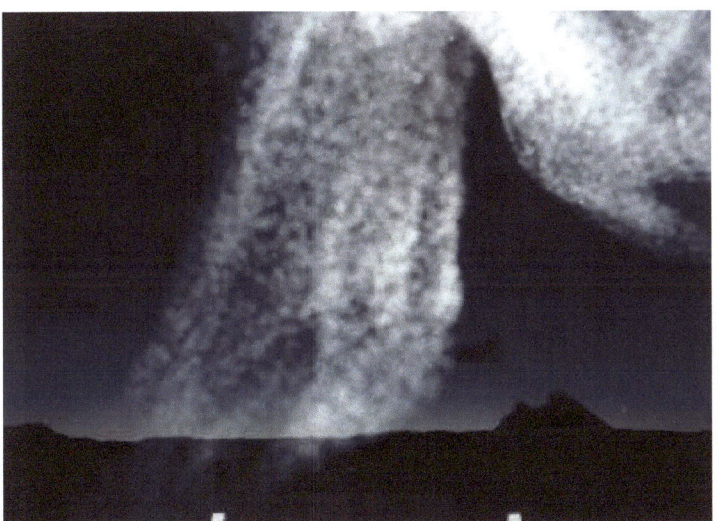 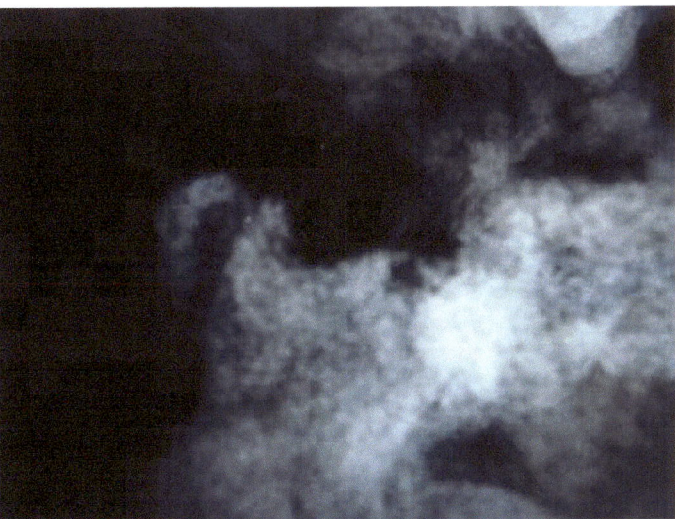

(Left) The wings of this swooping form show the texture of Circles. (Right) The blues most likely produced by the light of a full moon contribute to a crystalline effect of the Circles making up this picture.

Another anomaly that occurs in Circles is a subset called "Bounded and Rounded". While this does not occur often, it provides significant forming in what appears to be human-like shapes. The example below was taken in the spring of 2011 in front of the 120-year old farm house when leaves were just appearing on the trees.

This photograph titled Personage of the Myst, a Circle texture that is Bounded and Rounded, displays the beauty of nature and the Myst coexisting in the stillness of the night.

POCKED

A texture that is close to Circles represents a shift of focus to dark circles or spots circled by light rather than the light circles forming and shaping. This is what we refer to as **_Pocked_**. In this texture, while defined by the light, the dark spaces are prominent.

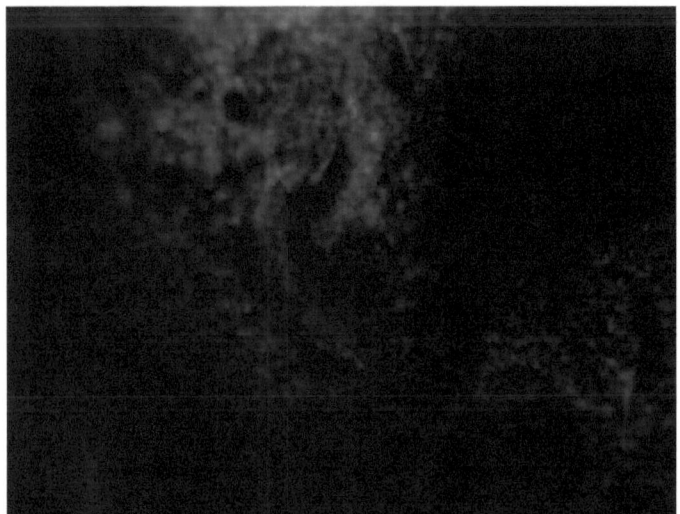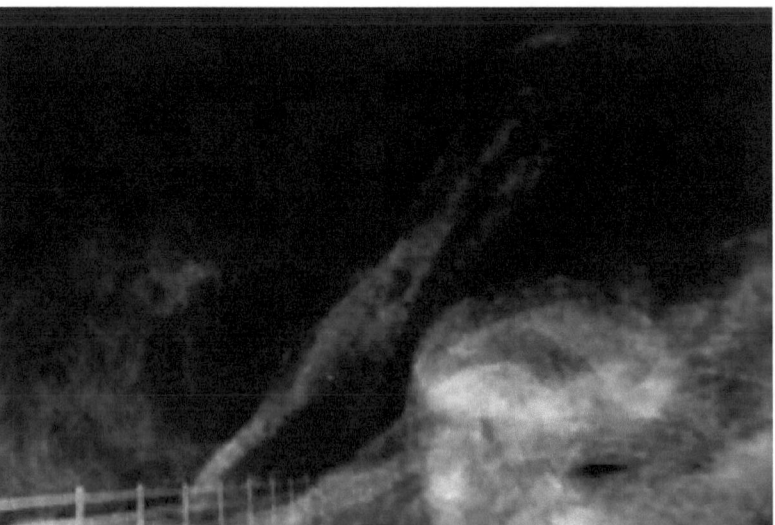

(Above) Here is an example of a Pocked texture (middle part of picture). (Right) A second example of pocked with additional color (see middle shape and parts of shape to right, which has accents of Cloud and light striations.

One example of the effectiveness of this reversal of focus is a photograph Alex took which reflects the shape of a dark dog. In January 2010 David and Alex lost their beautiful Akita, Sashi, who was black with a white ruff, four white paws, and a white tip to her tail. Alex has identified her face in both Pocked and Circle textures. See Chapter 6 on Interpretation and Meaning.

CLOUDS

The third major category of textures is **_Clouds_**. In Clouds the texture of the circles has softened to become continuous (or near continuous). While Clouds are punctuated and shadowed in terms of splashes of light throughout, they appear as a fluid whole, often producing a billowy effect. Many of the Cloud photographs are what Alex refers to as "Cloud Guides", which reflect the appearance of faces along one or more edges of the Clouds.

(Right) In this Cloud picture there are perceived faces along the upper edge. Note the interplay of light throughout the Cloud.

Clouds often present in color. Note the juxtaposed energies with clear faces both to the left and above the cloud.

* * * * *

Alex:

When the *Myst* began to come regularly in the Fall of 2010, there were evenings where it was glorious, surrounding me with the instantaneous emergence of a brilliance of white, displaying patterns too large for me to fathom in the split second I had to see them. So, I began to use two cameras, trying to produce a near-continuous field of visibility. While wonderful to the point of tears, the pictures that were produced were splashes of textured white with no clear boundaries in terms of form and shape. While those pictures were certainly more interesting than pictures of visible fog taken on other evenings (which were exciting in terms of discovering bright orbs mixing with the molecules of water!), they did not provide a way for me to further interpret and explore meaning.

So, one night early on I said to the *Myst*, "If this is for me, you've got me. This is a glorious experience. But if I'm to explore this further and to share this, I need to be able to clearly see and study in my pictures the forms and shapes you are taking. Can you form and shape in a smaller way, and try to come within a few feet in front of my camera?"

As the nights passed and the *Myst* pictures continued, I discovered that I needed to "remind" the *Myst* occasionally to form and shape in front of my lens rather than the flash. I began to believe that this had something to do with the different "feelings" I was having about various *Myst* energies. Sometimes I felt the *Myst* was quite familiar (even supportive and loving), while other times I sensed things such as curiosity, humor, and even a sense of protection with strong connections to the earth on which I stood.

Thus, it appeared that different energies were responding to me on different nights.

* * * * *

Like Circles, groups of Clouds display various subsets of characteristics. One grouping is defined in terms of "Splash". These are Clouds that are not defined within the picture by external form and shape, that is, no specific external boundaries were picked up within the picture. Cloud splashes are exhibited in many pictures taken early in *The Journey into the Myst*. Alex attributes this to the fact that the *Myst* originally presented quite large and surrounded her such that from her viewpoint it was difficult to perceive shapes and boundaries.

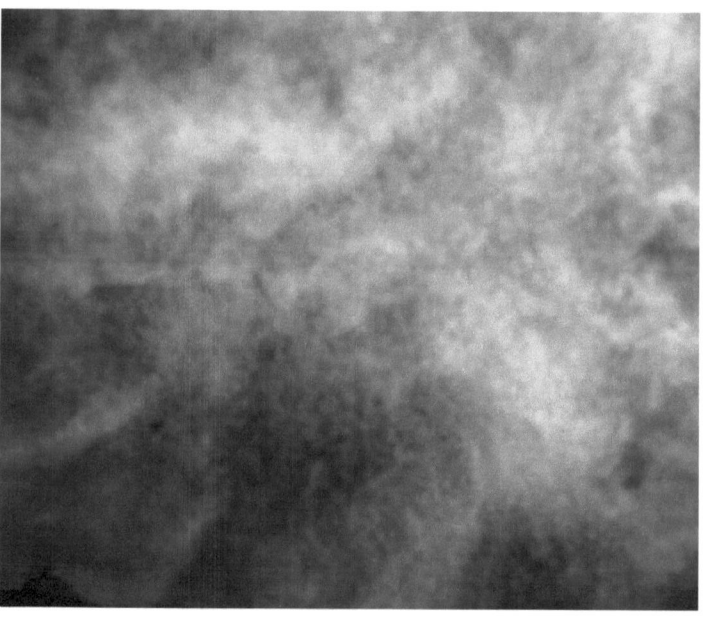

(Right) This Cloud Splash is filled with swirls and light accents. Although the lack of external boundaries makes it impossible to determine shape and form, faces can often be located within a Cloud Splash.

Some Clouds have anomalies described as "Swoops". These bright streams of light curve, providing the illusion of dancing through the otherwise formed Cloud of swirls. They are often helpful in perceiving shapes within the clouds. Swoops also form the basis of forms and appear in combination with other textures, sometimes creating the form itself for our investigation. Several examples of Swoops are pictured below.

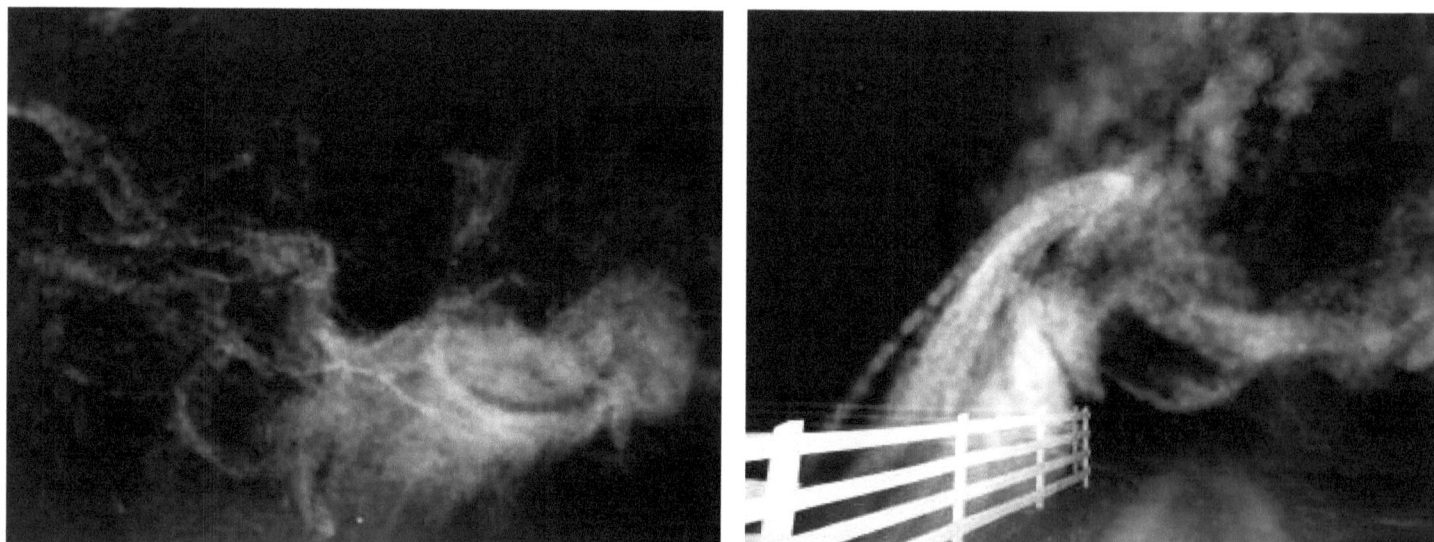

(Left) Swoops move through Pocked and Cloud textures. (Right) A Swoop moves into the Cloud texture, giving the context of movement, and causing the viewer to reflect on the possible faces in the upper right of the picture.

Similar to Circles, Clouds also form shapes that are Bounded and Rounded, often taking a human-like form, although the internal texture is clearly Cloud. And, we would be remiss not to bring up a subset of Clouds we describe as Ruffles and Wings. There are a large number of pictures that capture the edges of forms and shapes that fit into this descriptive category, defined with a sense of fun and to provide pictures for future reflective thought. (Pictures at the top of the next page.)

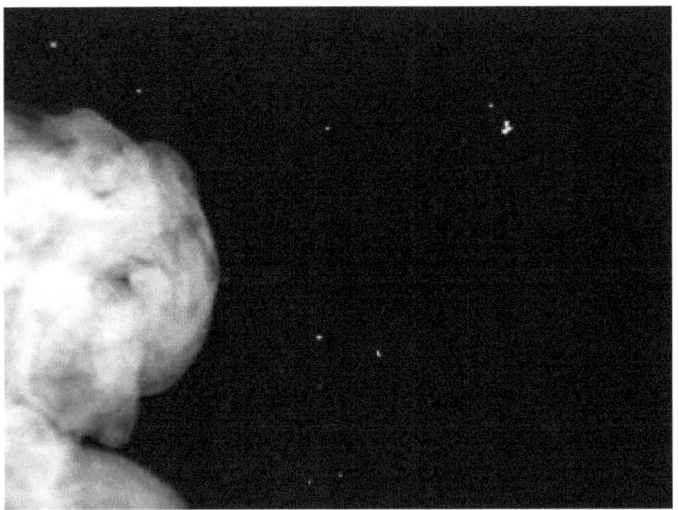 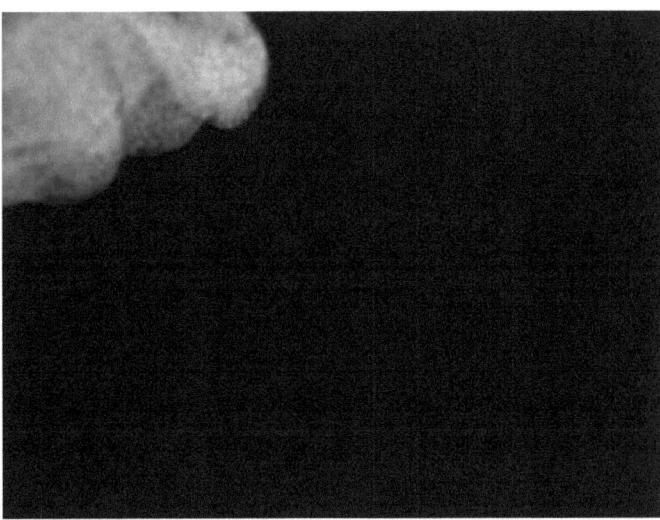

(Left) This delightful Bounded and Rounded Cloud picture is accented by small flakes of snow. The texture is Cloud moving toward Fluff (see below for a description of Fluff). (Right) This is the first definitive picture that was described in terms of Cloud Ruffles and Wings. Can you imagine the possible shape of the figure that goes with this wing?

FLUFF

There are times when the word "cloud" does not do service in terms of a descriptive term of continuous *Myst*. **Fluff** is far removed from the Circles characteristic described above. It is reminiscent of cotton candy, with a large number of soft light swirls, often accented with an inner clarity of shapes and forms. Fluff occurs when there is an ease of *Myst* flow, that is, when the energy is high, and Fluff is often accompanied by the appearance of pink areas throughout a *Myst* form.

A wonderful example of Fluff is the picture that represents Kumo, our tri-colored Akita dog that passed in the Fall of 2010. This story was shared in *The Journey into the Myst*. The picture is repeated here to demonstrate texture. The whites and pinks swirl and overlap, punctuated by small bursts of light and forms and shapes within the larger form.

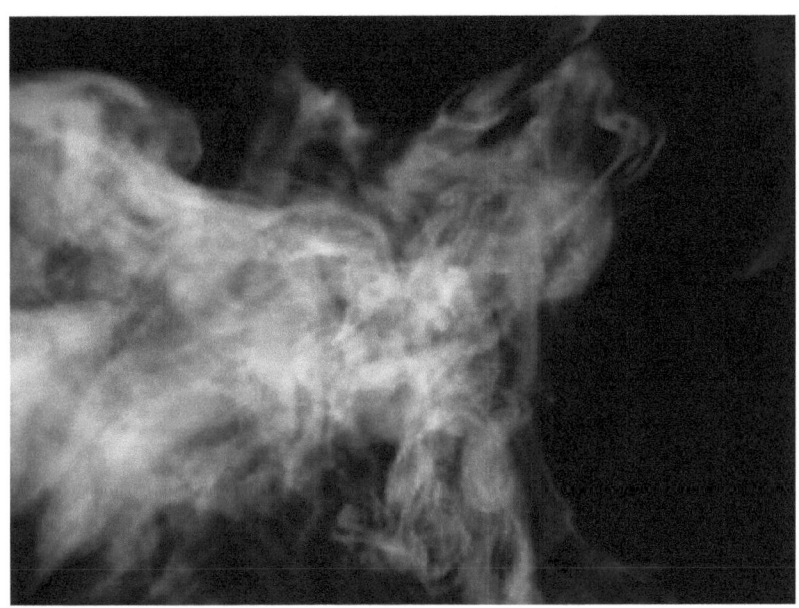

Fluff, especially when accompanied by other textures, is perhaps the most delightful to the eye in terms of beauty and ease of form, often including Swoops. Embedded in the exquisite *Myst* flows are layers of smaller faces and forms.

(Right) This picture titled "Friends of Light" is described in the Gallery as "Coming or going—ever with us—love is always close at hand" represents an excellent example of Fluff texturing.

DOTS

In some of the *Myst* pictures, there is the wonderful surprise of an explosion of energy conveyed by the appearance of small dots of light. The dots may or may not take a shape and form that is recognizable. Because these pictures occurred more rarely than other textures, they held a fascination for David.

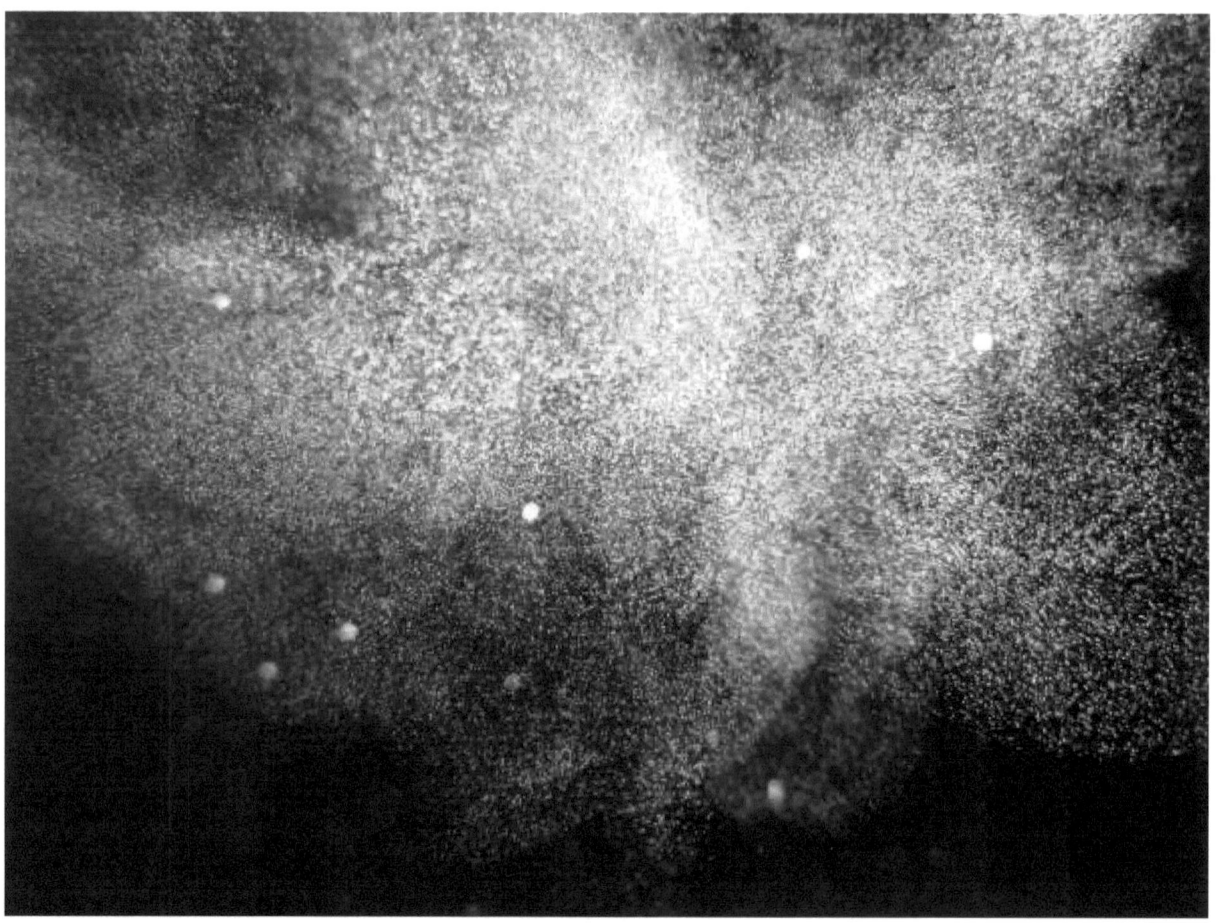

This amazing explosion of Dots is accented by bright orbs. This photograph is titled "Starburst" in the Myst-Art Gallery, with the description: "Like grains of sand in a storm, millions of Myst dots splay across the nighttime sky." Note the orbs as accent points.

* * * * *

David:

I find dots interesting because they appear to be independent and individual, yet they are close together and form overall shapes. Perhaps they are small spheres (orbs?). This is possible, but what ties them together? What forces are involved and how do they make boundaries? In some ways, they remind me of star groups or clusters. If they were truly independent, then they would most likely drift away from each other. When they first began to appear, they attracted my attention in terms of both their micropatterns and their macro patterns.

* * * * *

(Above) A swirl of dots in the picture above is enlarged to the right, where orbs appear to have a dominant presence in the formation. The pixilation does not allow clarity for further enlargement.

Dots can also take the form of Bounded and Rounded, that is, Dots that make up bounded and rounded shapes. In the example below, note the consistency of shaping across different textures of the *Myst*.

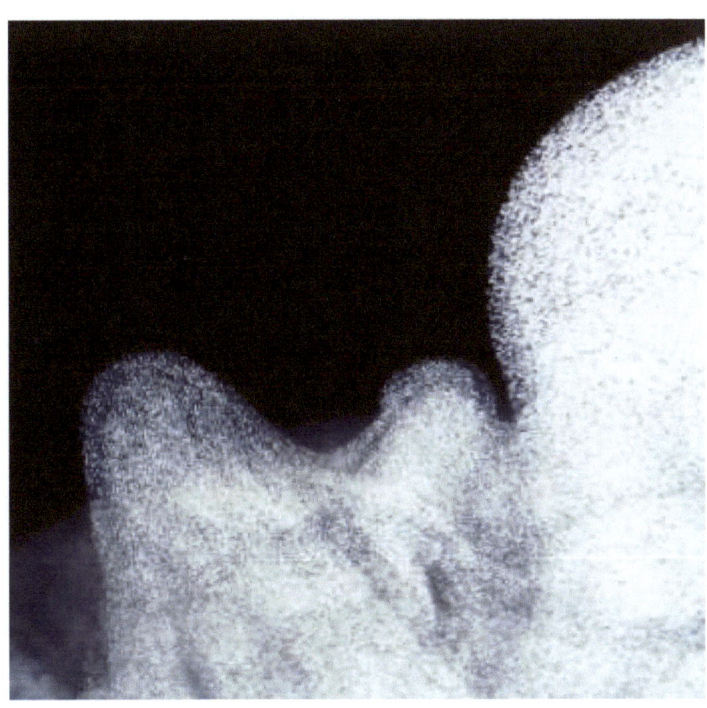

It is interesting that there seems to be a binding around the edge of the Bounded and Rounded forms, that is, there is a ribbon effect that sometimes represents an increase in light (as in the picture above), and sometimes presents as a decrease in light (as in the picture to the right). Additionally, there are lines within the larger forms which differentiate smaller forms. Again, these present as light or dark. Note that while there are certainly similarities in patterns, no two *Myst* pictures are the same. Each is unique.

(Right) This picture of Bounded and Rounded dots is titled "We are With You" and is described in the Myst-Art Gallery as "Veiled figures shaped from tightly woven dots of Myst stand guard through the night." If you look closely, you can almost perceive a face behind the veiled form to the left.

SQUIRMS

A texture variation of Dots is Squirms, although we treat them here as a separate category. These became discernible with an 18.2-megapixel camera, and only a few pictures fitting this descriptive category have been taken. Some of the earlier pictures described as Dots might well fall into this descriptive area if we were able to look at them more closely.

Squirms are reminiscent of looking through a high-power microscope at bacteria or the very beginnings of life. When these are blown up on the screen many of them have the appearances of faces, that is, darker spots where the eyes would be and characteristics that could infer one or more of the following: nose, mouth, forehead, hair, etc. In one picture of this nature, Squirms appear to overlay other textures, specifically, Cloud with a Soft Light area.

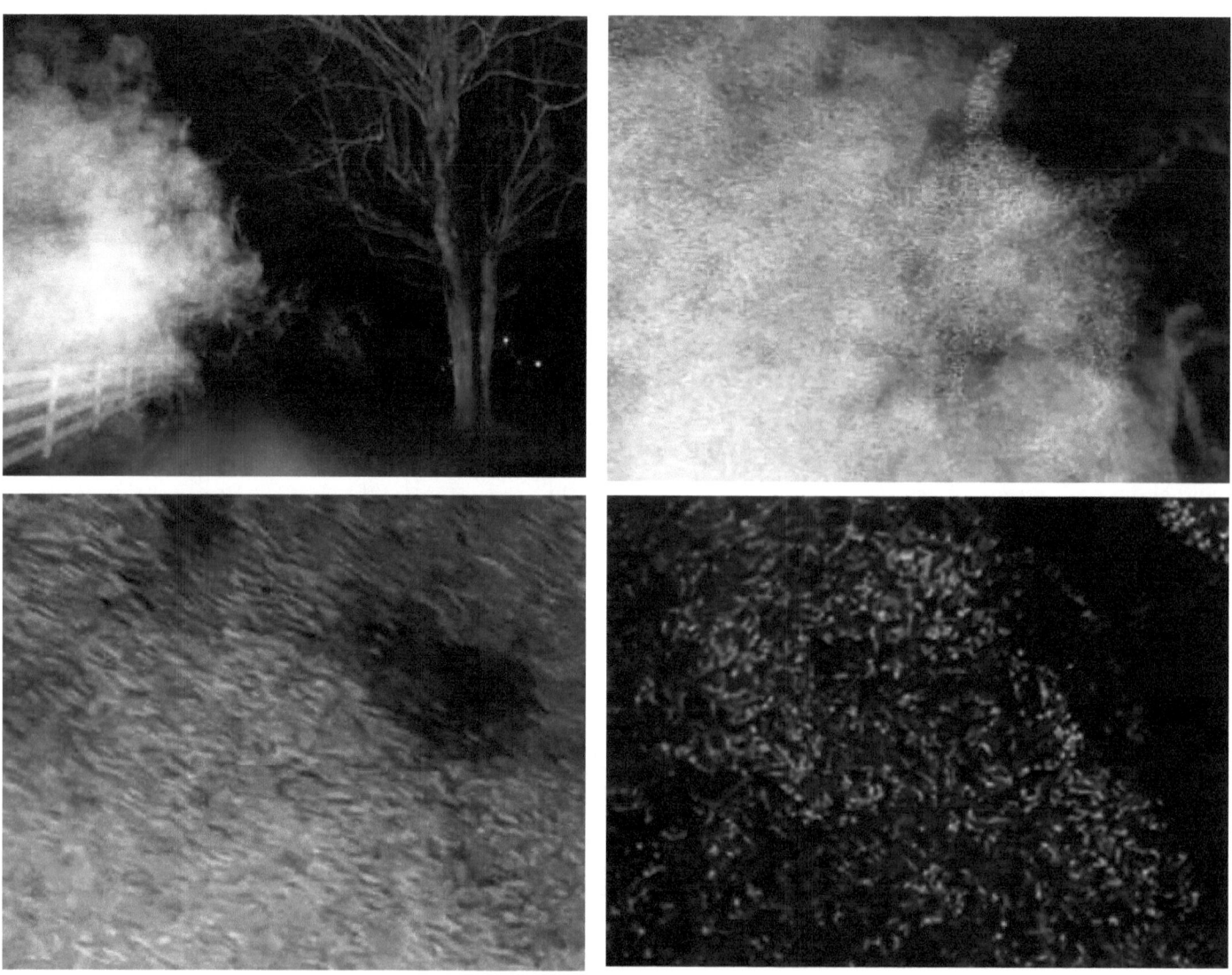

(Upper Left) This is the full picture as taken in November 2012. The approximate middle of the Myst form (Upper Right) is enlarged again (Lower Left) to show the Squirm texture overlaying a Cloud texture. The final picture (Lower Right) in this set is an enlargement of the area to the bottom right of the lighter Myst form in the first picture. This shows the Squirm texture against the black of the night.

As a point of comparison, a different photograph taken one week earlier is shown below. While still using a 16.1-megapixel camera, Alex captured many *Myst* forms with the Dots texture. It is possible that some of these are actually Squirms, although there is not enough clarity in the pictures to confirm this.

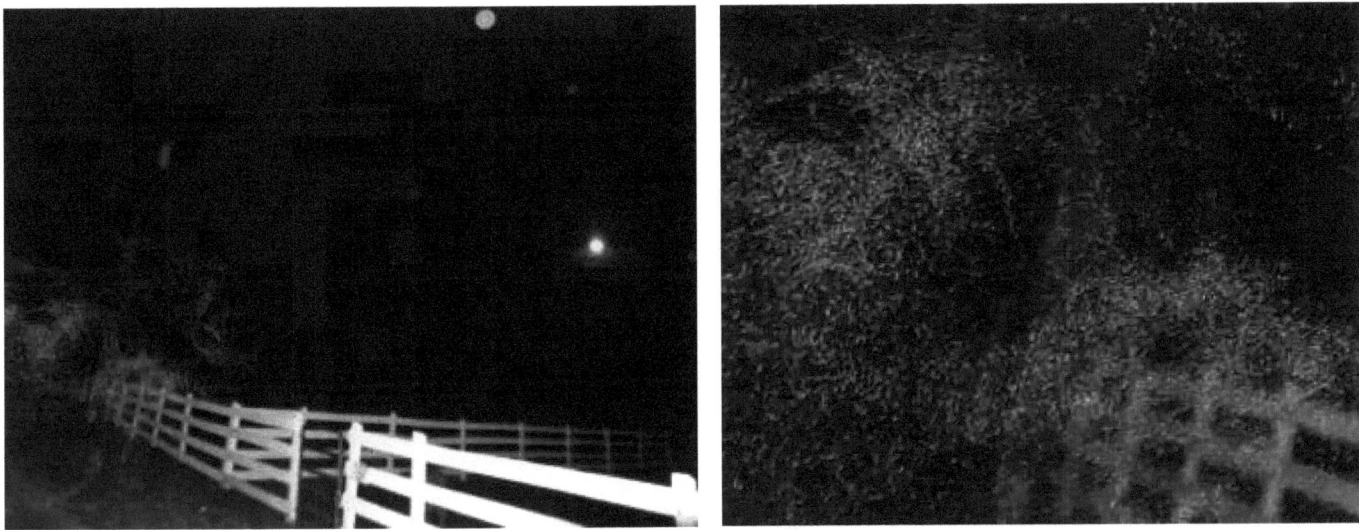

(Left) A photograph with Squirm texture taken in early November. (Right) The middle part of the photograph at the left magnified to show the Squirm texture (for reference, note the telephone pole).

Discovery of the Squirm texture caused Alex and David to review those more recent photographs (captured with the 18.2-megapixel camera) displaying *Myst* forms with a Dots texture to ensure that the Squirm texture was a separate phenomenon. The pictures reviewed showed a higher level of organization that appeared to relate more closely to the Orb shapes. One example is displayed below with several magnifications provided.

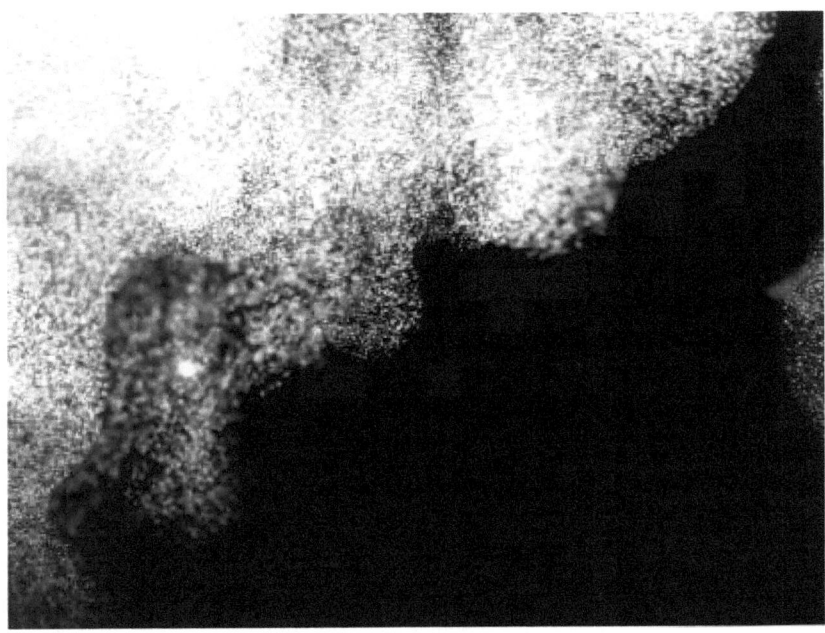

Photo taken November 2012 with an 18.2-megapixel camera that displays the Dots texture.

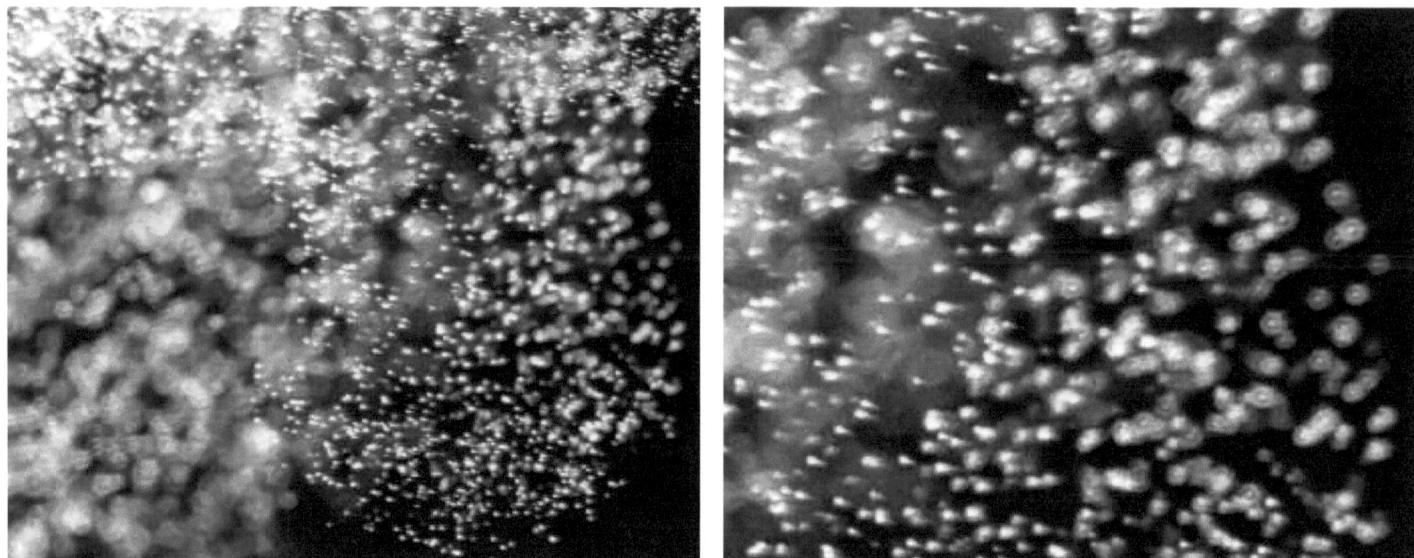

(Left) A magnification of the center part of the November 2012 photo on the previous page, and (Right) a third photograph further magnifying the upper part of this photo. These Dot textures (over Circles) are quite different than the Squirm textures displayed earlier.

That being said, three other possibilities came to mind. First, that these are different energies presenting. Second, that Squirms represent a higher density of energies. Third, that the Squirm phenomenon is a different stage of the process of the forming and deforming of the *Myst*, specifically, with an emphasis on the possibility that the Squirm texture occurred when the *Myst* is breaking apart. All three of these are certainly possibilities.

Diving even further, let's magnify the top and middle parts of the photo to the upper right one more time. While it will be a bit fuzzy, take a close look at the "orbs". Do you see faces?

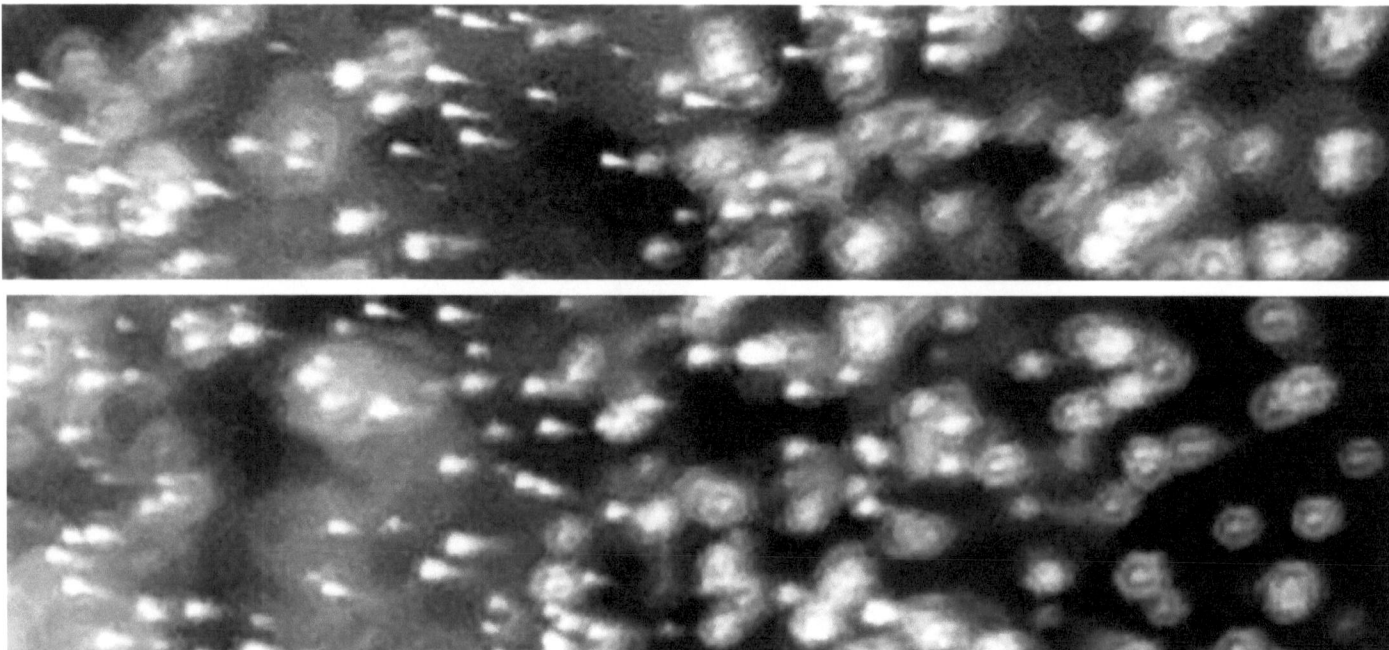

SOFT LIGHT AND BRIGHT LIGHT

Soft Light and **Bright Light** are something different, a shift off the continuum that may connect the other textures. While Soft Light and Bright Light can often be thought of as characteristics often associated with various textures of the *Myst*, periodically they define the texture itself. This is more often the case with Bright Light.

We begin with Soft Light. There is a surreal aspect to Soft Light pictures, a specific glow that emerges in parts of—or in all of—a specific picture that separates it from other Cloud and/or Fluff pictures. While Soft Light generally slides in between Clouds and Fluff, it can appear in *parts* of pictures primarily expressing other textures such as Dots. Perhaps we could refer to this aspect as a "highlight" in the picture. To better portray this there are several examples provided below.

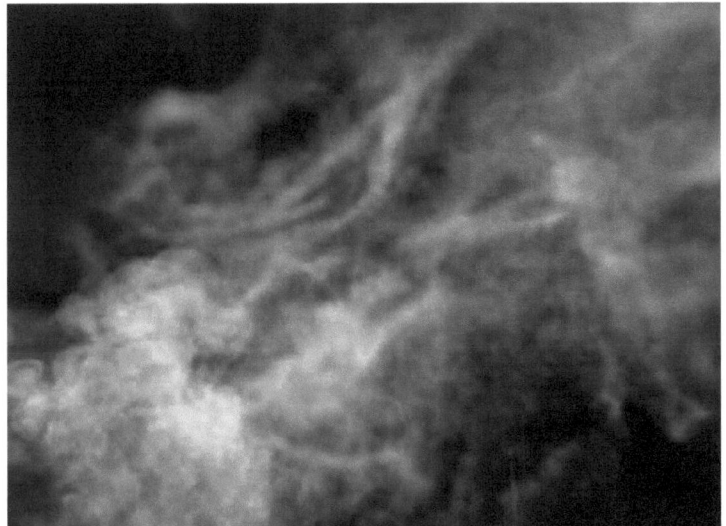 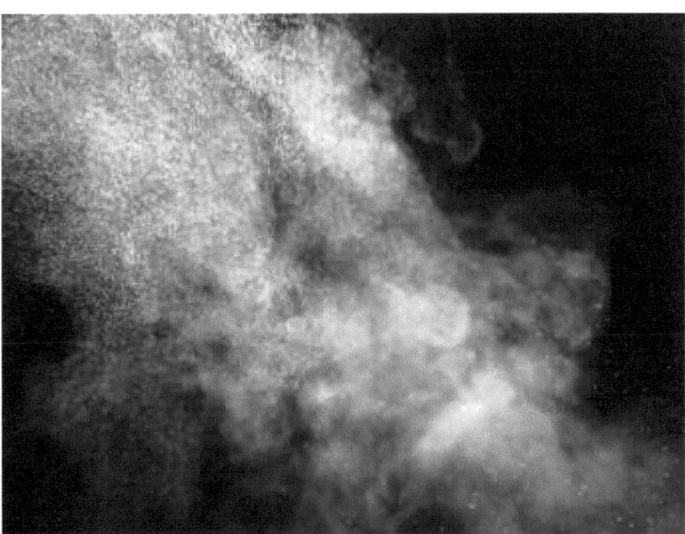

*(Left) This Soft Light Picture is titled "Drama in the Night" and is described in the Myst-Art Gallery as "A depiction of the Council in the Myst observing the struggle between good and evil." While the picture above displays aspects of Clouds and Fluff, it also generates a **glow** that moves the texturing beyond the normal Cloud or Fluff texture. (Right) A combination of Soft Light with a spray of Dots.*

Bright Light is a phenomenon that produces too much light for the camera to pick up the characteristics within a bounded shape in a specific picture, thus the texture of that part of the picture can be defined as Bright Light. Alex perceives this as much more than a forming and shaping of materials and energies at hand. Rather, she perceives a presencing of energies vibrating at a much higher frequency.

When it is raining or snowing, all the orbs become "Roy G Biv's" with the colors (red-orange-yellow-green-blue-indigo-violet) presenting around bright white centers. The spectrum of color in visible light is a gradation of wavelength from long to short, of frequency from low to high. Since the Bright Light *Myst* generally presents much larger than orbs, imagine the amount of energy required for that presencing. The camera, of course, can only pick up the shape by capturing what is *around* the Bright Light *Myst* form, although occasionally there are subtle indictors of characteristics *within* the Bright Light form.

In the first example provided below, the Bright Light shape occurs at the top of the frame. While this picture was taken just prior to sunrise, Bright Light shapes have been captured throughout various photographs at different times of the night. The second picture below shows a close proximity of the Bright Light phenomenon with the photographer. Look closely. does the light outline a face from the side? An excellent example of Bright Light is the picture entitled "Mother of Mercy, Angel of Light" featured in Chapter 8.

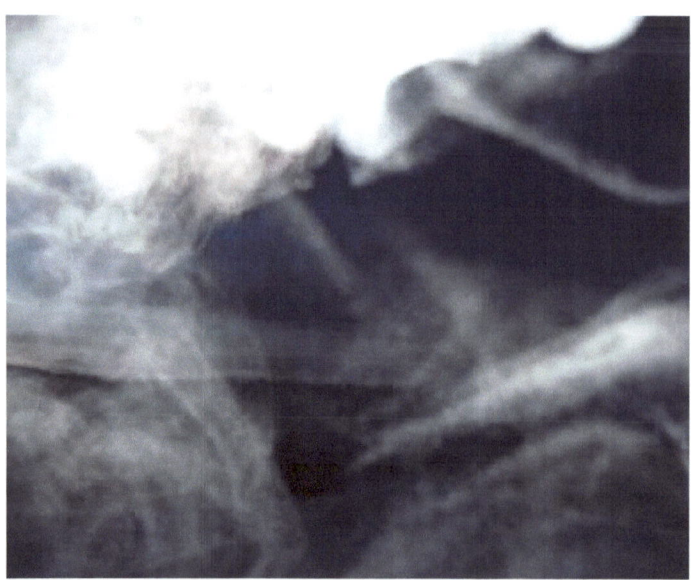 

(Left) This Bright Light picture is accompanied by tendrils of Fluff. (Right) Bright Light residing close to the photographer shaping the features of a face from a side viewpoint.

Within other photographs, Bright Light also appears as what is called "Light Striations". These Light Striations may be elongated, turning and twisting in various shapes. At the top of the next page is a picture with Bright Light appearing as Light Striations set in Fluff. As an exercise in pattern recognition, see if you can count the number of "arrowheads" that appear at the end of swirls of light within this picture. Note that "arrowheads" were often used to define the end of a dragon's tail(s). As a point of reference in exploring meaning in this photograph, here is a 2013 photo that shows a tail ending in an arrowhead. This photograph does not include Bright Light, indicating a lower level of energy presencing.

(Right) An "arrowhead", also widely recognized as a dragon's tail. (Compare with the photograph on the opposite page.)

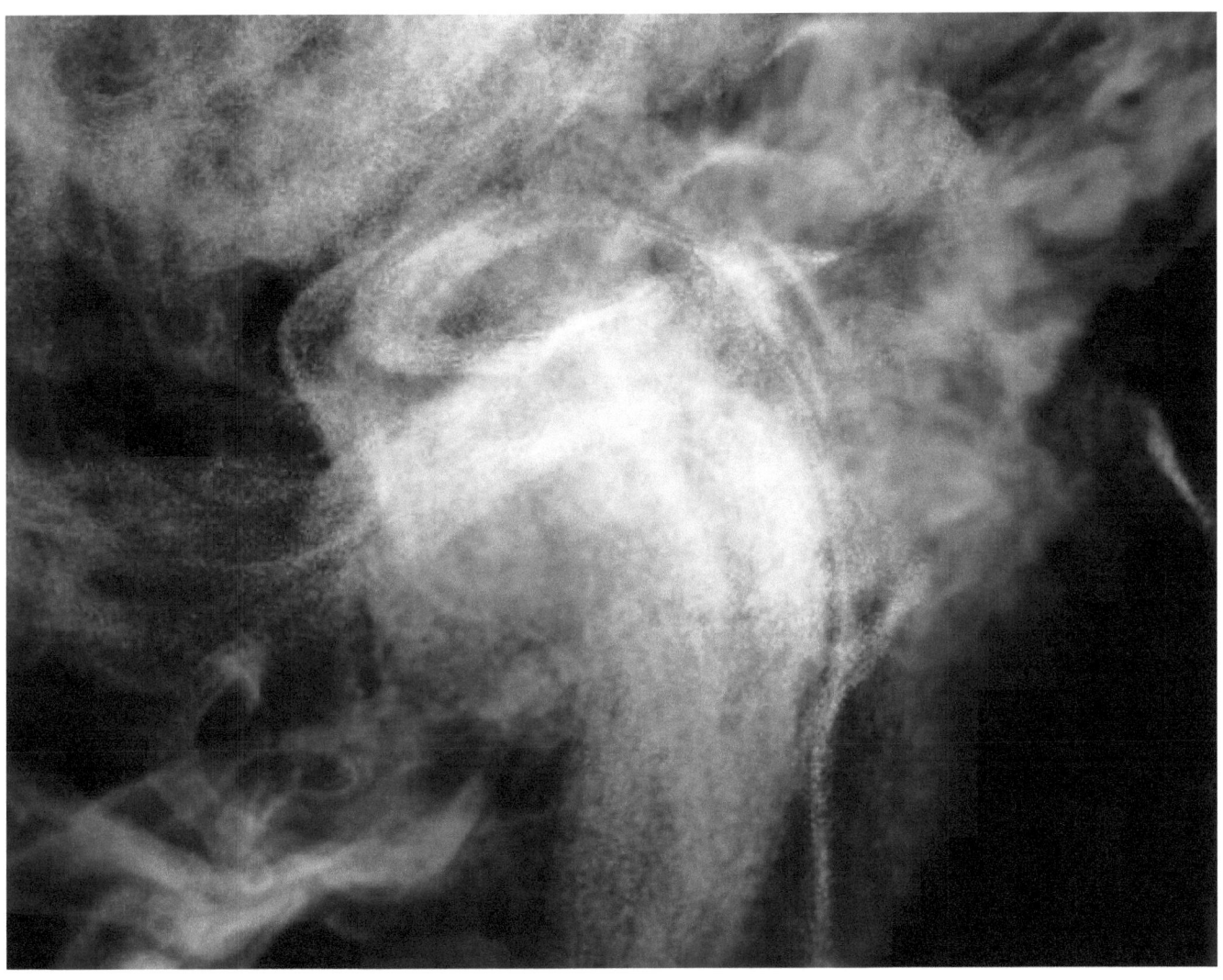

Bright Light appearing as Light Striations set in Fluff. This picture is titled "Dance of Light" in the Myst-Art Gallery with the description: "Miraculous mysteries of the swirling Myst caress the velvet of the night."

IN SUMMARY, there are roughly seven high-level descriptive categories for the *Myst*: Circles, Pocked, Dots, Squirms, Clouds, Fluff, Soft Light and Bright Light. These seven categories can be broken down into subsets as follows:

Circles	(Subsets: *Crystalline* and *Bounded and Rounded*)
Pocked	
Clouds	(Subsets: *Slash*, *Swoops*, and *Bounded and Rounded*)
Fluff	
Dots	(Subset: *Bounded and Rounded*)
Squirms	(Can be an overlay on other textures)
Soft Light	(Often in combination with other textures)
Bright Light	(Often in combination with other textures)

Before leaving our discussion of textures, it is significant to note that different textures of energies, each part of a form with boundaries, can be juxtaposed in the same picture frame or instant. Some earlier photographs where this occurred were with Clouds and Dots. This is, at some level, a validation that the phenomenon is far beyond the ability to pick up dust particles or vapor trails in the night sky. First, if this were true, they would appear in picture after picture, which does not occur with the *Myst*, which requires building a resonance. Second, the energies in the frame would be similar, not differentiated by shape/form/texture/color, etc. But let's not jump to conclusions. There is more to explore in terms of patterns.

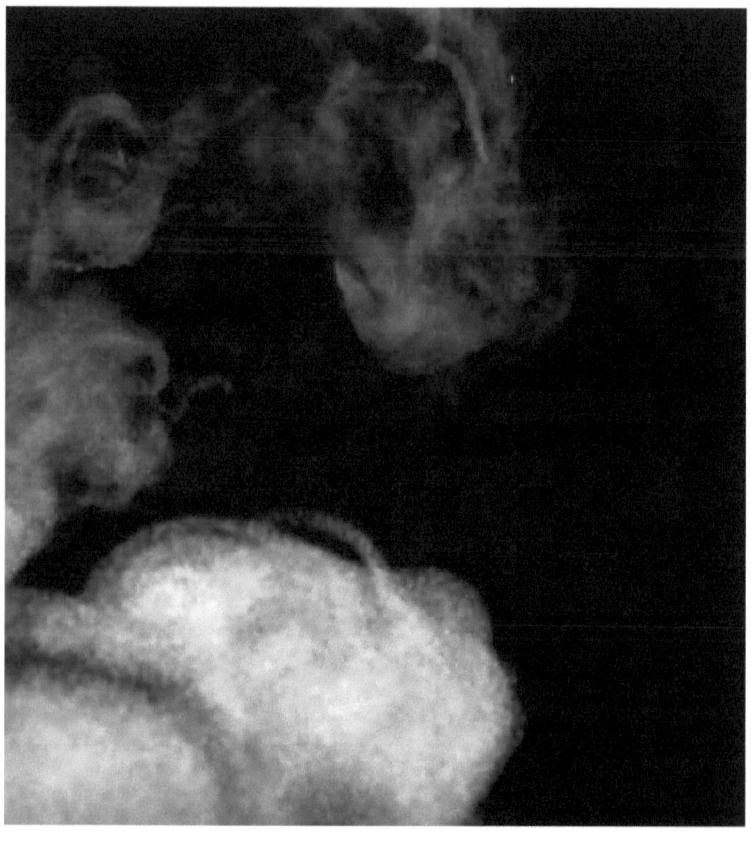

The picture to the right is another example of different energies appearing in the same camera frame. If you use a bit of imagination, you can almost see that there is a conversation underway among these energies. I wonder if we are the subject of that conversation?

Building on our earlier discussion of patterns in terms of form and shape, it is important to reflect on the role that color and texture may take in our interpretation of, and subsequent assignment of, meaning to the *Myst* photographs.

It is possible that the textures of the *Myst* are what could be described as **levels of energetic involvement of the orbs**. Recall that the sphere is the most useful shape for the conservation of energy.

(1) We start with the orbs that expand and come together to form and shape a larger essence presenting as Circle forms with the circles still clearly seen. Pocked is a variation on Circles, with an emphasis of dark circles instead of light circles.

(2) As the energy builds—or when there is immediately available a higher level of energy—the circles become less prominent and present as Cloud forms, though often retaining Circles around the edges of the Cloud forms.

(3) As the energy continues to build—or when there is immediately available an even higher level of energy—the *Myst* takes on the characteristics of Fluff, light dancing energy with graceful curves and twists. At the Fluff level it may be that the *Myst* is being influenced by other electromagnetic energies than the orbs, although pictures of orbs have been caught playing around all of the textures of *Myst* forms.

(4) As the energy builds even higher—or when there is a very high level of energy available—the *Myst* bursts into a fireworks of Dots, holding shape and form but conveying the beauty and magnificence of birth and potential.

(5) Squirms, a shifting of energy, may present the unforming process of the *Myst* forms.

Chapter 4: Patterns of Response

What is it about this phenomenon that causes the *Myst* to respond to Alex? Obviously, this is unclear, but we **can** explore the internal and external aspects of the situation when this occurs. External aspects include specific location, environmental conditions, and periodicity of communication; internal aspects include mental and emotional constructs. We will also consider the resonance between the participating energies, Alex and the *Myst*, sharing the communication approaches that emerged and end by describing an evening of play.

EXTERNAL AND INTERNAL CONDITIONS

Alex has captured Orb pictures around the world along with the inevitable scattering of water molecules and dust particles in the air. The focus of this book is the *Myst*. While most of the *Myst* pictures have been taken at the Mountain Quest location, Alex has also captured *Myst* pictures at two other sites. The Mountain Quest Institute is located on a high valley farm in the Allegheny Mountains of West Virginia. This is a country setting amidst a large acreage of National forests. The location is unique in terms of being part of the "quiet zone", that is, the farm is located in a 40 square mile zone surrounding the National Radio Astronomy Observatory housing the Green Bank Telescope which observes and studies radio frequency signals from space. There are no cell phone towers in this area because they would cause interference with the telescope, which is designed to handle a great range of wave-lengths from 9 feet (3 meters) long down to 1/8th inch (3 millimeters). Thus, the Mountain Quest site is a close-to-nature setting in terms of the atmosphere around the land as well as the farmland and undeveloped forestation.

The other two sites where Alex has taken *Myst* pictures are also located in the mountains. One site is The Monroe Institute[5] (TMI) in Farber, Virginia, which is part of the Blue Ridge mountain range. The facility is located on the top of a mountain. When Alex spent a week at TMI's retreat site, she was able to capture *Myst* pictures every night. The third site is a rest stop about half way between Harrisonburg, Virginia, and Frost, West Virginia, again at the top of a mountain. Each of these sites is exclusive in terms of a natural setting and surrounding vegetation offering the opportunity for Alex to interact with the *Myst* without other people around. As a point of reference, Alex has unsuccessfully attempted to bring in the *Myst* while traveling in Brazil, Ecuador, France, Portugal, Singapore and Thailand, although the settings have not been comparable, that is, these were not the mountain settings in nature where she has been able to photograph the *Myst* in the United States. Further while abroad she was not in the same frame-of-reference (creating resonance) nor did she have the time to prime the settings.

A primary external consideration is the weather. Through journaling Alex was able to better understand the weather patterns when the *Myst* would be more prevalent. While Alex has been able to get a *Myst* photograph in warmer temperatures, there is an ease of appearance that occurs when the temperature drops below 50 degrees Fahrenheit. Generally speaking, there is a balance between temperature and humidity, that is, when there is a high level of moisture in the air from a recent shower or storm a 50 degree or lower temperature is not necessary to get *Myst* pictures. While *Myst* forms **can** appear in the air during a light rain, and easily appear in the snow, if there is more than a slight breeze no *Myst* forms appear. Thus, the ideal environment would be a still night with 50 degrees Fahrenheit (or below), with snow adding an exciting element that facilitates the appearance of the *Myst*. This is discussed further in Chapter 9 on the Physics of the *Myst*.

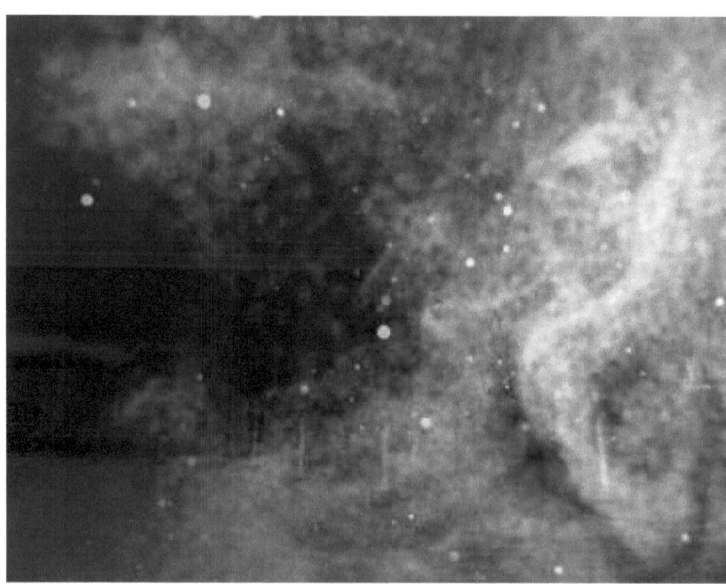 

(Left and Right) Orbs and the Myst dance with the snow.

The internal environment comes into play here as well. Most often Alex has completed a meditation prior to her excursions outside. While *Myst* pictures can be caught in the light of day (and some of these are available in the *Myst*-Art Gallery), Alex prefers to see the *Myst* forms more clearly as they appear to her eyes in nighttime photography. Of note here is a reference that appears over and over again in Alex's journal. So often she is caught up in the beauty of the night sky, with the Milky Way stretching across the middle of the sky directly overhead often accented by a "shooting star." The journal reference is to "feeling" that she can reach the stars, pull them down to her, and questioning their relationship to the beautiful orbs that accent the *Myst* pictures. The question becomes: Is this "feeling" about the night sky part of the resonance that has been created by the situation?

RESONANCE

Resonance is an exchange of energy between two people, two systems, etc. that is facilitated very efficiently because of the way it is exchanged, the rate it is exchanged, and the amount that is exchanged. **The phenomenon of resonance occurs when "things" exchange energy back and forth at a rate which is comfortable (most efficient) to both.** For example, if one was trying to exchange three times a second and the other at four times a second, they would not be in resonance. A good example of resonance is when a baseball pitcher and catcher are working closely together in terms of their timing, motions and anticipation of the other's actions. Minimum energy is used and the "system" achieves maximum capability. In Alex's case, the resonance is most likely felt by Alex as an intense internal joy and close relationship with her surroundings and, in particular, with the *Myst* itself.

Resonance is a physical phenomenon, with each action having its own frequency. Theoretical Biologist Bruce Lipton talks about resonance in terms of the lipid extensions coming out of cell walls. There are approximately 200,000 lipid molecules extending out of each cell, each one different than the other and reacting to different external frequencies and forces. One of the ways they communicate is through natural frequencies that are resonant with each lipid. For example, when an external chemical has a resonant frequency near a specific lipid's resonant frequency, then the lipid will allow that energy into the cell. This results in a flow of information into the center of the cell that then takes away the sheath protecting a specific part of the DNA, allowing the DNA to be expressed. If an external chemical is NOT resonating at the same frequency as the lipid, then nothing will happen. So, the frequency of a chemical represents the combination used to get through the door of a cell wall.

How is resonance being produced in the *Myst* phenomenon? One possibility for producing frequency is Alex's singing, with the acoustic vibration impacting the molecules of *Myst,* with interaction depending on the frequency of the sound, the effect on the *Myst* and/or perhaps some effect on the intelligence behind the phenomena. Another aspect most likely has to do with the emotional system. When a human is feeling love and joy chemicals are flowing through the body which can actually transmit in the air (through smell, etc.) and may have the potential for triggering atoms in the *Myst*. Another possibility for producing frequency resonance is the energy produced by the flash of the camera. The *Myst* reflects back the camera's flash, showing different textures and patterns. This is certainly connected to the phenomenon.

Finally, we must also consider the possibility of entanglement (building on the non-locality experiment) causing instantaneous response across long distances. While highly improbable, this is offered here as a possibility. This would require much more research to validate.

THE POWER OF INTENTION

Intention is the source with which we are doing something, the act or instance of mentally setting some course of action or result, a determination to act in some specific way. It can take the form of a declaration (often in the form of action), an assertion, a prayer, a cry for help, a wish, visualization, a thought or an affirmation. Perhaps the most in-depth and focused experimentation on the effects of human intention on the properties of materials and what we call physical reality has been that pursued for the past 40 years by Dr. William Tiller of Stanford University. Dr. Tiller has proven through repeated experimentation that it is possible to significantly change the properties of at least one physical substance by holding a clear intention to do so. His mind-shifting and potentially world-changing results began with using intent to change the acid/alkaline balance in purified water, later experimenting with consistent success on liver enzymes and the development cycle of the fruit fly. The ramifications of these experiments have the potential to impact every aspect of human life.

What Dr. Tiller has proposed (Tiller, 2007) is that there are two unique levels of physical reality. The "normal level" of substance is the electric atom molecule level, what most of us think of and perceive as the only physical reality. However, Dr. Tiller proposes that a second reality exists that is at the magnetic information level. While these two levels always interpenetrate each other, under "normal" conditions they do not interact; they are "uncoupled." Intention changes this condition, causing these two levels to interact, or move into a "coupled" state. Where humans are concerned, Dr. Tiller states that what an individual intends for himself with a strong sustained desire is what that individual will eventually become.[6].

Tacit Knowledge and Intention. Most likely those who are reading this book are familiar with *The Secret* and perhaps with the work of Jerry and Ester Hicks and Abraham, the source of the ideas for *The Secret*. What was not forwarded in *The Secret* was the knowledge that we live in a vibratory universe. Intent is directly correlated to our vibration, but it is not just the intent of our conscious mind. The authors have done considerable research and writing in the area of knowledge. We have defined knowledge as the capacity (potential or actual) to take effective action. The term "tacit knowledge" is used as a descriptive term for those connections among our thoughts that cannot be pulled up from memory and communicated in words. We may know what decision to make or how to do something but we cannot describe it from memory in a manner such that another person can extract and re-create that knowledge (understanding, meaning, etc.).

Tacit knowledge is held in the unconscious and can be considered in terms of embodied, intuitive, affective and spiritual. *Embodied* tacit knowledge is represented in neuronal patterns stored within the body, and is both kinesthetic and sensory. Kinesthetic relates to the movement of the body and sensory relates to the five human senses through which information enters the body (sight, smell, hearing, touch and taste). *Intuitive* tacit knowledge is a form of knowing created within our minds (or hearts or guts) over time through experience, contemplation, and unconscious processing such that it becomes a natural part of our being. *Affective* tacit knowledge is connected to emotions and feelings, with emotions representing the external expression of some feelings. *Spiritual* tacit knowledge can be described in terms of knowledge based on matters of the soul. The soul represents the animating principles of human life in terms of thought and action, specifically focused on its moral aspects, the emotional part of human nature, and higher development of the mental faculties (Bennet & Bennet, 2007, 2008b).[7]

While informed by Spiritual, the Embodied, Intuitive and Affective tacit knowledges are local expressions of knowledge, that is, directly related to our expression in physical reality. Spiritual tacit knowledge is our relationship with All That Is (Source, God), recognition of and participation in Oneness or Unity Consciousness. Connecting Tiller's model of intention with the Bennet model of tacit knowledge, it begins to become clear that effective intent relates to an alignment of the conscious mind with the tacit components of the mind and body, that is Embodied, Intuitive, and Affective tacit knowledge. We have to know it, feel it, and believe it to achieve the coupling of the electric-atom-molecular level and magnetic information level of physical reality.

While the *Myst* was unknown to Alex in the beginning of her experience, once it began to appear her expectations and passion built. As described below, she began to set the intention to interact more fluidly and understand the responses more clearly. Once she had seen the *Myst* and, given supportive environmental conditions, the *Myst* consistently appeared, and there was an increase in Alex's **expectation** that the *Myst* would be there when it was called (both conscious and unconscious: a knowing, a feeling, a believing). That expectation, driving intention, increases the probability of response. Thus, intention sets the stage for moving into a "coupled" state of physical reality, directly impacting interaction with the *Myst*.

Acknowledging this relationship of intention and reality, we must consider whether it is the photographer/viewer that is setting the intention or another intelligent source, specifically, the source that forms and shapes the *Myst*, or some combination. This leads to another series of questions (always more questions!) Is it the *Myst* that we are influencing or are we influencing whatever is behind the *Myst*? After the first point of recognition, no doubt it is both. Is the intelligent source behind the *Myst* represented by the orbs? We do recognize that the orbs are in relationship with the *Myst*. Recalling that the whole phenomenon of the *Myst* began with a joyous summer of Orbing with Alex always asking for more, then the *Myst* would appear to be the response to that intent.

This same understanding of the power of intention carries over into the process of pattern detection. When Alex and David search for faces, sure enough faces are there in many photographs. When these are pointed out to others, those others seem to see the faces as well. Are the faces there outside the seeing and pointing out? In our understanding of conventional physics, the answer would be yes. But as we transition to a new understanding of physics in terms of a magnetic information level of reality, which no doubt plays with the ideas of Quantum, there may be no separation between the intention and the thing that appears. Much research and consistent, independent and repeatable experimentation is needed before this will be accepted as scientific fact.

INTERACTING WITH THE *MYST*

As shared in *The Journey into the Myst*, in the early days of the *Myst* at Mountain Quest Alex asked some deeply personal questions and was rewarded with *Myst* photographs that provided answers, howbeit with a high level of interpretation involved.

In her second wave of communication, Alex worked out a system to ask "yes/no" questions. She asked the *Myst* (or the intelligence behind the forming of the *Myst*) to come directly in front of her camera if the answer to a question she asked was YES; and to move away and not appear in her camera if the answer was NO. She would repeat this process three times for each question to ensure that the response she was getting was non-random. Further, following three answers that were the same, Alex would validate the answer by asking the *Myst* to do the opposite of the answer, that is, if the answer to the question was YES (*Myst* in the picture), she would ask the *Myst* to GO AWAY for her next shot (number 4), and then COME BACK into her picture on shot number 5. Thus, it took five pictures to ensure that each answer was correct and validated as a non-random pattern.

Alex was able to ask a variety of questions, although it was always difficult to remember them when she was in a "joy and flow" state, and, frankly, in that state the questions didn't seem very important. Further, the difficulty of remember questions to ask may be caused by the tacit intention needed to sustain communication with the source of the *Myst*. Many of the questions Alex DID remember to ask, and the answers to those questions, have been shared in the first book. But not all. Since we are moving into interpretation and meaning in this book, perhaps this is the place to share another story about those question and answer sessions. Since this story is sensitive to a religious context, this will be shared in Alex's words.

* * * * *

Alex:

Somewhere along the process I built up the courage to ask some burning questions about this man named Jesus. First, was there a real person who we call Jesus the Christ? The answer was YES. Somewhat relieved and recalling the answer to my earlier question about reincarnation, I quickly asked, "Was I alive during that time?" The answer was YES. Getting up close and personal, I sang out, "Was I related in some way to Jesus?" The YES answer took my breath away.

Thoughts tore through my head. I was there when Jesus was alive AND had some relationship to him! I could hardly contain my excitement. Did I dare ask? Should I go for the whole enchilada? Building up my courage, I asked, "Was I one of the Mary's?" And here came the YES, NO, and AWAY FOR 5 SHOTS sequence, while through my head ran the words, "If you were Mary would you be living this life now?" There was what I perceived as laughter, and I laughed with them. My guides always seem to have a sense of humor, even in response to serious questions. Then the words in my head continued, "If you were Judas, it would destroy you. If you were a member of the crowd and did nothing, you would be disappointed. Is there really an answer to this question?" I reflected, my head now in silence. Any answer would certainly have impacted my self-perception and emotional system this time around. They were right: No answer was the right answer.

This was the first time answers occurred quite distinctly in the form of words/thoughts ringing in my head.

* * * * *

After about six weeks of this question and answer interaction with the *Myst*, Alex began hearing all the answers in her head before she asked the questions. Surprised, she stopped the question sequence. How could she have external validation when she was hearing internal responses? Again, Alex and David began to question how much of this external phenomenon Alex was creating, or at least influencing. Did it exist without her in the picture? [Pardon the pun.] This was answered as she discovered others were able to get their own pictures, and did. The question now became: Were we as humans producing this external phenomenon?

There is no doubt both the orbs and *Myst* are responsive. Given conducive weather conditions (not too windy and stormy), the orbs were always there when Alex sang, her heart full of love and joy, asking them to come into her picture. The *Myst* might take a bit longer at times, but again, given conducive weather conditions and the properties needed to produce the *Myst* (a balance between temperature and moisture in the air), the *Myst* always appeared when Alex sang, her heart full of love and joy, asking them to form and shape.

An almost full-time participant in this process was Cat Walker, a feral cat who decided Alex was his person. There was a picture of him in the first *Myst* book, striding across the yard with orbs following behind and above. Throughout the years, Cat Walker would choose to come over to Alex every night she was taking pictures and jump into her arms, full enjoying the picture experience. And, frankly, since he is quite large, he would sit balanced against her shoulder for an hour at a time, purring as Alex sang and flashed.

As she began to share the experience of the *Myst* more freely with others, Alex's connection of this phenomenon with love and joy was repeatedly confirmed. Those individuals with a light, playful attitude, able to fling off the trials of the day and live in the now, were the ones who were able to bring in the orbs—and sometimes the *Myst*—for themselves.

AN EVENING OF PLAY

In life we are the producer, script writer, director and actor. We also play primary, support and understudy roles in the lives of others. And from the looks of the *Myst* pictures there is a cast of extras numbering in the millions or higher. This was never clearer than on an evening in the Fall of 2011 when Alex asked the *Myst* to move through the Mountain Quest Institute's three-acre corn maze to create some interesting pictures.

It was the night before the grand opening of the first corn maze at Mountain Quest. Alex's son Andrew had taken this on as a special project, combining it with FrostFest, a local fair held on the grounds of the Institute. When Alex let David know of her intentions to photograph *Myst* in the corn maze, David insisted that they walk over together. Alex had a penchant for not taking a flashlight, even when the night was quite dark, but on this occasion the flashlight was welcomed as they moved across the bumpy hayfield to the entrance of the maze.

David brought along his own camera and stayed at the entrance outside on the field as Alex moved into the maze. Alex stopped, let all the tension from the day go, and took a few deep breaths of love and light. Then she blew a bubble of light around herself and began to sing, asking the *Myst* to form and shape for her tonight. But she did not yet start shooting pictures; rather, she sang to the *Myst* about the possibility of getting some special pictures of the *Myst* playing around and in the corn maze. The *Myst* was incredibly responsive, fully posing per Alex's instructions. The story related to this experience will be told in the captions as the *Myst* pictures are shared below.

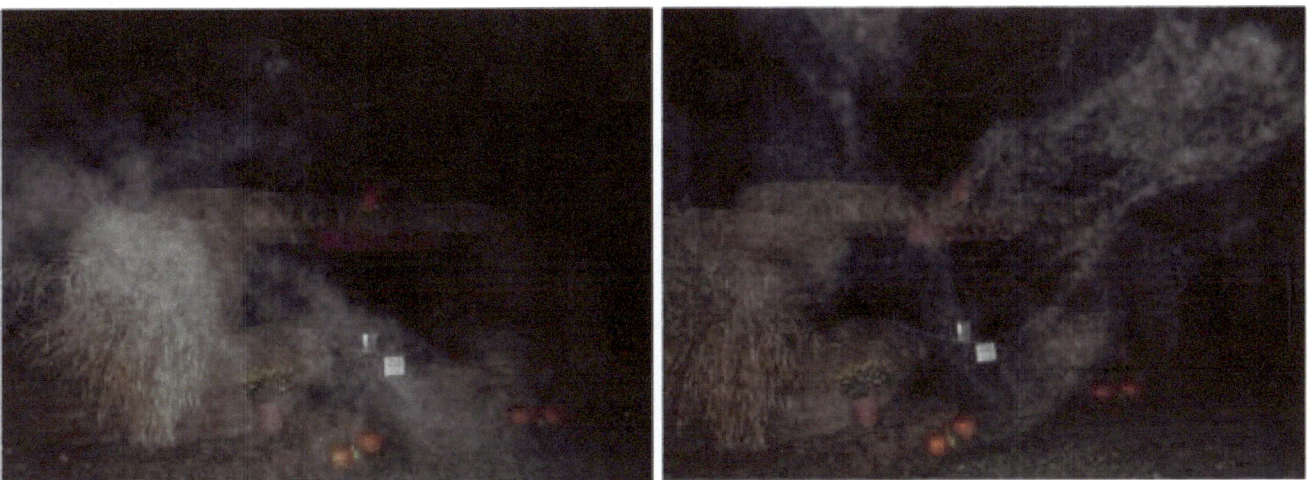

And into the maze they went. (Left) "Entrance" and (Right) "A Mysty Welcome". The Myst energies check out the chained entrance, but it doesn't hold them back!

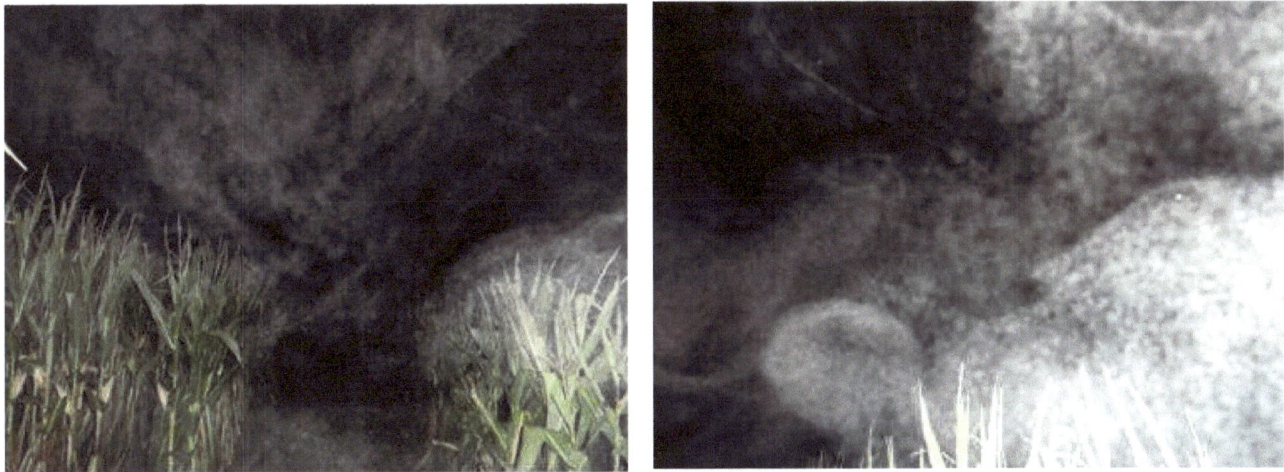

As the Myst moved about and Alex photographed, (Left) gliding through the corn it was sometimes too far ahead. "This isn't a race," Alex shouted. (Right) A tortoise appeared in her next picture.

(Left) But then, maybe it WAS a race ... (Right) at least the Myst was at the exit before Alex was!

When Alex walked to the exit David was patiently waiting. "I've been dialoging with the *Myst* in my imagination," he told her. Alex snapped a few pictures, and sure enough, David WAS dialoguing with the *Myst*.

This photograph is titled "Consultation" and described: "Night-time travelers confer to plan the haunted maze advertised for Halloween." Alex didn't shoot any Myst pictures during the haunted maze.

Exhilarated, with energy cursing through her body, Alex couldn't wait to see the results of the pictures. As she passed by the red and white fair tents, she snapped a few more pictures. Laughing, she paused by the hay wagon and asked her *Myst* friends if they enjoyed dancing on the hay wagon. The second picture below was the *Myst* response.

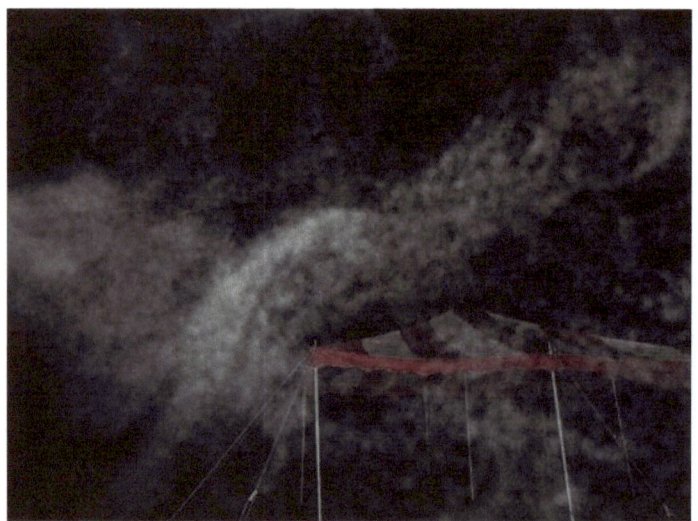 

(Above) This picture is titled "A Festive Spirit" and described: "The Myst celebrates the next-day opening of Frost Fest." As she studied these photographs Alex could not help but notice a similar slanted pattern of energy at the front of the maze, at the end of the maze and over the tent. (Below) This picture is titled "Light-Footed Dancers" in the Myst-Art Gallery and described as: The Myst taps a tune atop the hay wagon.

Several weeks later, now October, the new Air Evacuation Lifeteam helicopter serving Pocahontas County landed in the front pasture of Mountain Quest for an evening event held at the Inn and Retreat Center. As can be seen by the photo below, and in other photographs taken during this landing, the *Myst* took considerable interest in this new guest.

(Above) This picture taken on October 5, 2011, is titled "Wings and Props" in the Myst-Art Gallery.

Following scrutiny of the new Air Evacuation Lifeteam helicopter, Alex walked over to the nearby badminton net that had been set up for kids to play and asked the *Myst* if it would like to play badminton. Sure enough, the *Myst* "played" both sides of the net.

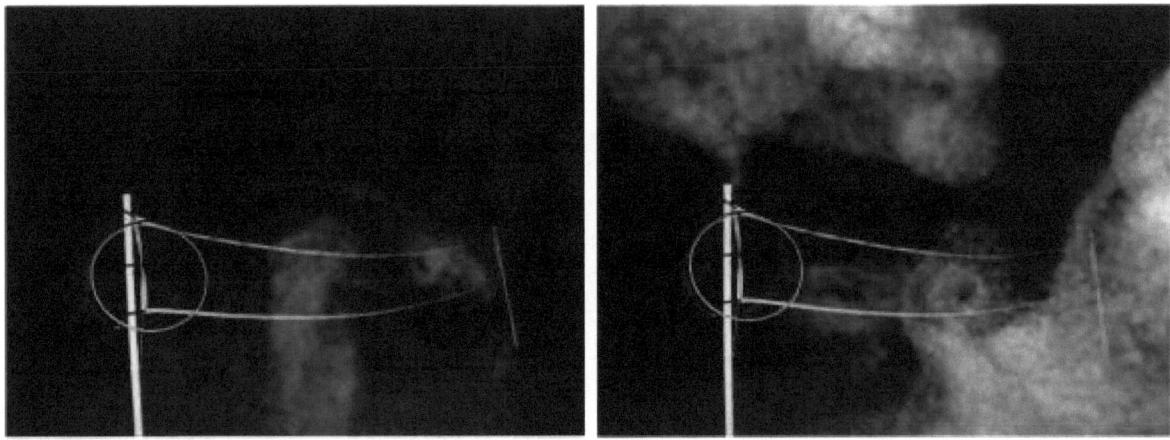

These pictures are titled (Left) "Over the Net, not Through It" and (Right) "Who's turn to serve?"

These wonderful experiences began a new process of interacting with the *Myst*. Alex began to realize that the *Myst* was NOT going away (a continuous worry for her that first winter), and that the joy and playfulness that she was experiencing was being reciprocated by her *Myst* playmates. **They were having fun too!**

Chapter 5: Patterns ACROSS the *Myst*

There is a thrill that occurs when patterns begin to emerge across *Myst* pictures, an exhilaration as forms in the pictures are connected to other forms/shapes that have become familiar over the weeks and months of exploring *Myst* photographs.

There are many approaches to identifying patterns, some of which will be discussed below. One generic approach that opens up the mind is to shift your frame of reference. For example, look at a picture from the viewpoint of your religious beliefs, from the viewpoint of a child, from the viewpoint of an artist, and from the viewpoint of the photographer. We're not looking specifically for meaning in this chapter, just the ability to identify patterns. Different viewpoints will often allow us to perceive different patterns.

* * * * *

Alex:

When I was exploring orbs over the summer of 2010, I began to notice similarities of specific orbs, or rather, the characteristics within Orbs which would repeat. Perhaps some of this was due to the fixation that occurred when I realized that there was a large number of animal faces appearing in the orbs. For example, once I saw a greenish colored Orb whose characteristics reminded me of Sashi [our black Akita dog who passed in January 2010], I then looked closely for those characteristics in every green orb that came into my picture, and often found them! However, this changed with the *Myst*, which actually formed and shaped from the asking! I know the power of intent, but could I REALLY be projecting this myself? That sounds a little more ego-centric than I prefer to think of myself, but certainly a consideration to be explored. We do create our reality ... but could I create a reality I hadn't perceived, a reality I didn't know existed? Or, is this about opening doors? So many questions, so many questions. So, I refocused on that which I COULD perceive, the patterns ACROSS the *Myst*, finding things that look alike, things that seem to have some sort of relationship to each other.

* * * * *

After the first few months there were enough photographs of the *Myst* accumulated to start looking a bit more closely at patterns across the *Myst* pictures. Similar to what was done with the orbs, Alex began to try and categorize the *Myst* pictures by content or what she perceived them to be. The categories and subcategories just kept expanding. For example, Angels stretched out to Angels, Angels Clear, and Angels Maybe. Guides morphed into Guides, Cloud Guides, Cloud Guides Clear, Cloud Guides Fluffy and Cotton Candy, then expanded to include specific descriptive terms for guides that appeared in multiples frames. These included Guide Animal, Guide Bony Large, Guide Curved Feet, Guide Curved with Face, Guide Hollow Eyes, Guide King, Guide Large Ears, Guide large Eyes, Guide Long Neck, Guide Moving Triangles, Guide Octo, Guide Phallic, Guide Pointed Face, Guide Polar Bear Guide Reptilian Guide Soft Pointed Face, Guide Whale and Guides Great Whites.

As the categories continued to expand, so did the number of photos saved in the "Unknown" file. It didn't take long for Alex to discover that it was impossible to categorize all of the *Myst* pictures. Further, the "Cloud Guides" and "Whispy" folders were so full they were pretty useless in terms of bounding and refining search parameters. In frustration, Alex stopped categorizing for a while, spending that time just looking closely at the photographs and noting special features she would find. Further, just the sheer number of photos now in her files was overwhelming. She originally was keeping ALL photos, even all the blank ones in between the *Myst* visitation, which showed that the phenomenon was not just there waiting to be photographed but actually responding to her call. Eventually, she concluded that it was okay just to keep one blank one, and that the number of the photographs would show the spacing; also, eventually, she began to delete wisps or a few orbs that did not clarify when enlarged.

ELEMENTAL ENERGY

Alex began to discover that periodically there was a welling of *Myst* energies that appeared to be coming up from the ground. These were generally not distinct in terms of shape, and the *Myst* appeared less dense, more opaque. It was one evening when David was out with her capturing *Myst* pictures that these characteristics began to make sense. As demonstrated in the photographs below, Alex was outside taking pictures and captured a picture of a tube-like *Myst* figure with what could be best described as a "happy face". Twenty minutes and 100 pictures later David joined her. Alex gave David the camera and asked him to take a picture of her calling in the energy. That picture of Alex shows what appears to be the "happy face" energy similar to that captured in the earlier shot communing with Alex, who laughingly said to David upon seeing the picture: "Now we know where the happy face came from!"

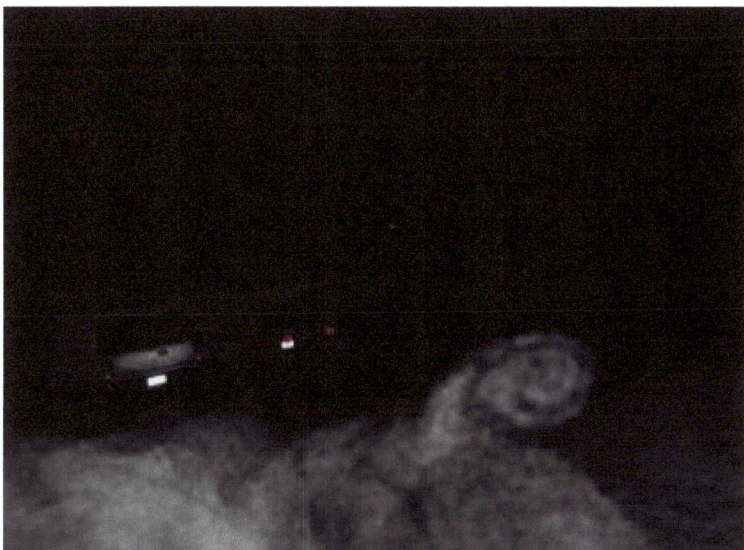 

(Left) This picture of "Happy Face" energy was taken by Alex. (Right) Twenty minutes and 100 pictures later, using the same camera, David took a picture of this same energy interacting with Alex. The pictures were taken in the same approximate area, but from a different direction, the first looking toward the garage, and the second looking toward the fenced horse field in front of the house and garage.

Since this energy was considered by Alex as having some connection to the Earth, she began labeling it "Elemental Energy." She felt that the "happy faces" are simple Elemental Energy, and that other energies that fall into this descriptive category are more developed, that is, presenting a more distinct form and less opaqueness but still appearing to be ground-bound.

Let's explore these Elemental Energies a bit further. For example, in comparing dozens and dozens of photographs in which they appear, taken on different days and, indeed, in different years, they primarily appear with the textures of Circles or Clouds, and rarely have they had elements of Bright Light within their boundaries. Further, they appear during all seasons of the year, so weather is not contributing to their texture; the picture to the right was taken during a light snow.

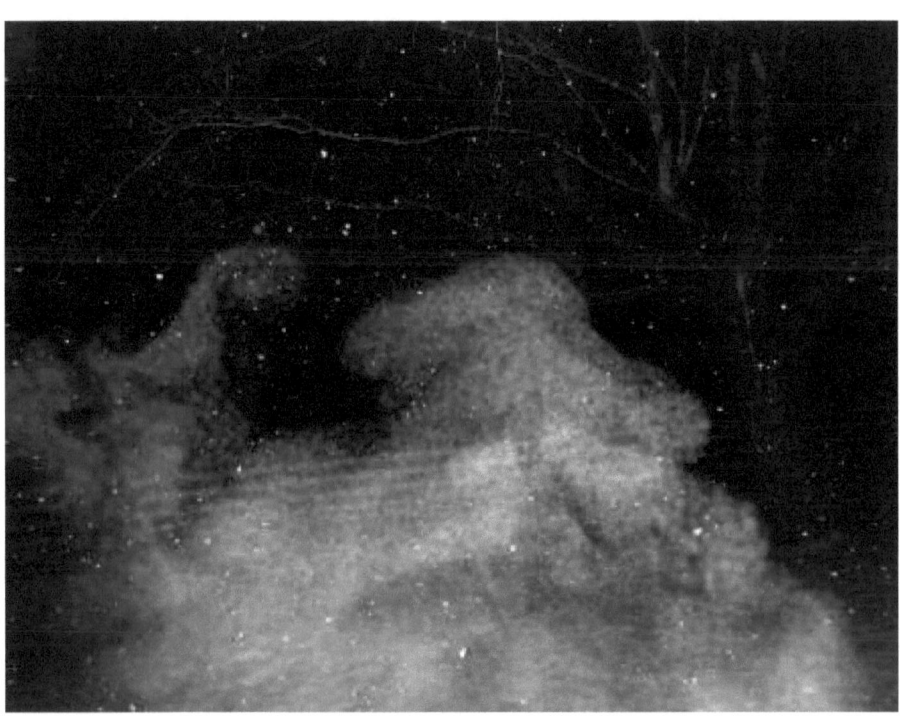

(Right) A conversation seems to be occurring, although the Elemental Energy to the left appears to be looking at the photographer.

Still grouped with Elemental Energies, are more developed forms, that is, forms who appear to have an upper body while very much remaining connected to the Earth. In inspecting multiple photographs, these figures almost always appear to be rising out of the ground, although several which appear at a higher level have had a *Myst* shape below them (cloud, etc.), which is sitting on the ground.

These Elemental Energies would often appear in photographs interacting with energies more free-flowing, or more Celestial in nature. For example, the photograph to the right appears to display a higher-order energy, and presents with Fluff. While rarely married with Bright Light, as previously noted, there is a whole series of photographs taken at Sunset along the front fence that present as these higher-order (in terms of shape) Elemental Energies appear in concert with other textured energies.

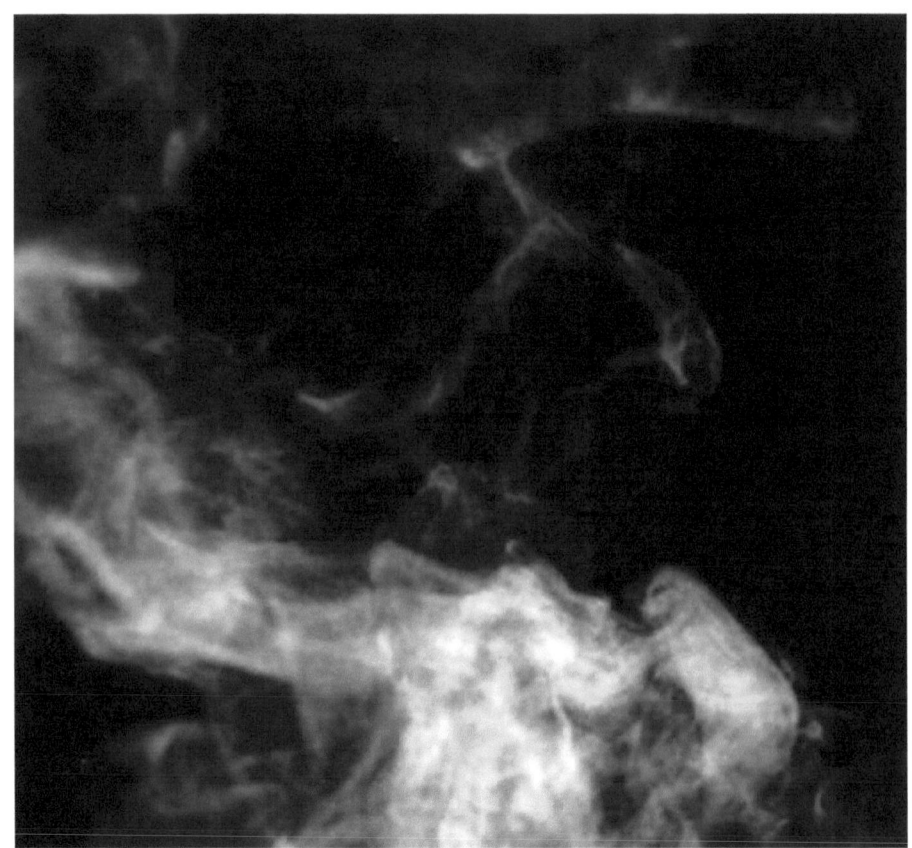

(Right) Higher-order Elemental Energies dancing together, with other energies celebrating the dance. Just imagine the possibilities for a moment being able to join in the fun. What are they celebrating? What would YOU be celebrating?

The photograph below titled "Evening Prayers" shows both Elemental and Celestial energy. This photograph was featured in the Preface of the first book in this series, *The Journey into the Myst*. This is also the picture that was displayed at the local fair, FrostFest 2010, for passersby to describe. While ranging from the idea of a cougar launching into the sky to "Mother Earth's evening breath", three that were more spiritual in nature were: (1) I see Jesus looking out into the night looking down at a child ... and dancing angels; (2) There is a kneeling figure praying to the Holy Spirit figure ... angels watching from above; and (3) Trumpets, angel wings, a woman praying, three angels, one with outstretched arms.

What is interesting about these three descriptions (the only ones more religious in nature) is that they all describe the energy to the left as a "higher order" energy. For example, in (1) Jesus is at the left, the child at the right; in (2) the Holy Spirit is at the left and a kneeling figure is at the right; in (3) an angel with outstretched arms is at the left and a woman praying is at the right. This is consistent with Alex's perception of Celestial energy at the left and earth-connected Elemental energy at the right.

In the Myst-Art Gallery, "Evening Prayers" is described in the following way: "As the sun goes down elemental earth energies connect with celestial possibilities over the fence to eternity." Additional descriptions of this photograph were contributed by individuals during a local event hosted at Mountain Quest called "FrostFest." These are included in the Preface of the first book in this series, The Journey into the Myst.

The energy in a similar photograph entitled "Supplication"—taken the same evening as "Evening Prayers"—shows a similar Elemental energy to the right of the fence. However, the energy to the left also appears to be earth-bound. The texture of this photograph is primarily Circles and there are several Light Striations moving through the center of the picture, one of which appears to demarcate a raised arm from the lower figure connected to the reaching forearm of the higher figure. The face of the lower figure is turned towards the photographer. The picture is accented by orbs, with a light blue orb near the center of the picture.

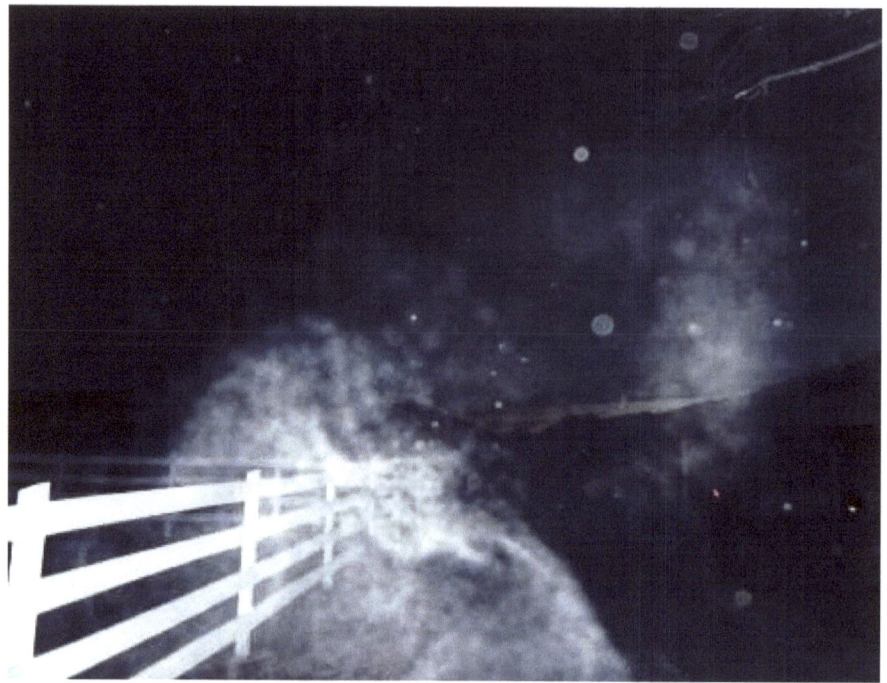

In the Myst-Art Gallery "Supplication" is described in the following way:
"A prayer of gratitude draws the energy of the orbs to fill the night sky."

FACES

While it is only natural that the observer would attempt to identify within the *Myst* that which is familiar (see Chapter 6 on Interpretation and Meaning), it is also undeniable that faces are presented in the *Myst*. Faces were introduced in the Chapter 2 discussion of non-random patterns. Of course, by now you have had the opportunity to look a number of pictures of which faces appear a part. Some of them are clearer than others.

In looking closely at a number of pictures—ones that were more *Myst* than form and shape—the question is often asked, "How do you really know those two dark marks are eyes? Maybe they are just random marks in rounded cloud edges." David's answer was, "They could be, of course. But if so, why are there repeatedly two dark areas and not three or four, and why are they spaced the way they are within those rounded cloud edges?" In fact, David does not recall ever seeing three or four dark areas spread relatively close together. Yet randomness would almost certainly come up with three or four or more dark circles in some pictures. So, the first clue in recognizing a potential face in the *Myst* is the "eyes". If we can find that pattern, it helps identify other possible features in relationship to the eyes.

The figure to the right in the photograph entitled "Look to the Skies" (shown below) is an excellent example of a figure with "eye marks" within a rounded "cloud edge". Of course, we are given a large hint in this one in the form of a second figure, to the left of the first, whose face below a head scarf is upturned, with a clear chin, the semblance of a nose and an eye, all in the places that make sense. The figure to the right, the one which serves as our example, is much less defined, yet still has a "mouth" mark situated appropriately. This figure also appears to be looking up, and from the slant of the mouth mark and tilt of the head there is a sense of fear conveyed. Bright Light appears throughout her head and upper torso area.

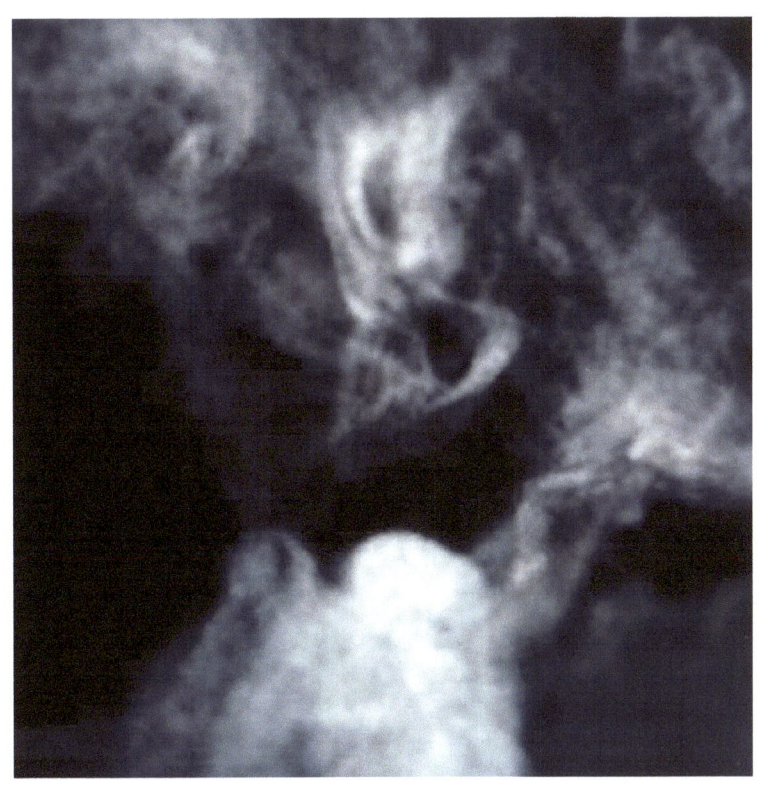

(Right) This picture titled "Look to the Skies" is described in the following way: "Fear? Look beyond the first impression to the essence of actuality."

The sense of fear is further accentuated by the flying figure above whose feet seem to be reaching for the lower figures. With a bit of studying, you can perceive a dragon's face with fire coming out of the mouth. The texture of the picture is Circles and there are several Light Striations helping to form the diving dragon's head. There is also a soft accent of pink, particularly in the *Myst* forming the dragon. What is curious is that there appears to be a smiling face just to the left of the perceived dragon's face, leading you to wonder about the true nature of fear.

Now, recognizing "face" patterns more clearly, we begin to realize that some of the faces appear to have special defining hats of some nature. This was true with the two figures in the photograph above who appear to have scarves or head coverings. Another example is the round face in the photograph below that has a crown atop his head. This picture is cropped from the larger picture "Crowned with Light" which is presented in Chapter 8. This crowned face has subtly appeared in more than 20 *Myst* photographs. The primary texture of the photograph is Fluff accented with wonderful pink swirls.

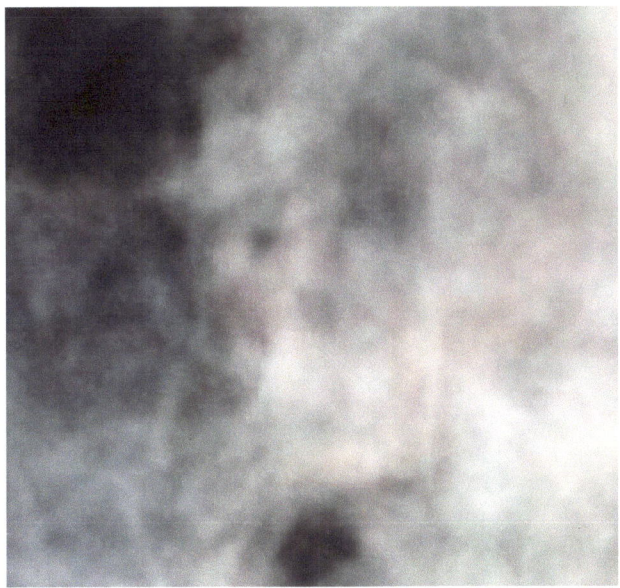

(Right) Near the upper left is part of a round face topped with a crown. Note the subtle, perhaps more feminine, face to the upper right of the crowned face.

The picture at the bottom of this page is titled "Approaching Night" and is featured on the cover of this book. The face appears to be surrounded by a scarf or burka. Note that the left hand of the *Myst* figure is lifted to the brow just above the left eye. In this picture the brows, nose and mouth are visible, as well as a chin line. She (assumed) appears to be wearing a coat trimmed with fur around the wrist and a glove, both of which are visible on the raised left arm. While the right shoulder and upper arm can be imagined, the lower right arm is not discernible. The figure is in a sitting position, although there is nothing visible that she is sitting upon. The fun question becomes, who/what is that swooping form with whom/which she is interacting? The look on the face is one of reflection moving toward slight bewilderment, if there is such a concept. Certainly, there is some questioning in the face. Since there is no fear evident, the swooping, conversing form may be present to either help or observe. Does this swooping form have a head/helmet, and is that possibly a cape swooping up and off the shoulder?

Let's look at color and light. There is a brighter stream of light bending from the right center to the bottom center (or vice versa). The two figures are not paying any attention to this light … or are they? Could the light be the subject of the sitting figure's gaze? While the sitting figure is somewhat opaque, there is pink interspersed in the *Myst*. The swooping form has pink up the front and around the shoulder area, but there is no pink in the head/helmet area.

Texture? Definitely Cloud in nature with part of the "cape" of the swooping form moving toward fluff, but not quite. There is a Light Striation coming down the top of the brighter stream of light in the lower part of the photograph. orbs float around the pair, with a light blue Orb situated on the front of the head/helmet of the swooping figure, perhaps near where the eye would appear if there were an eye.

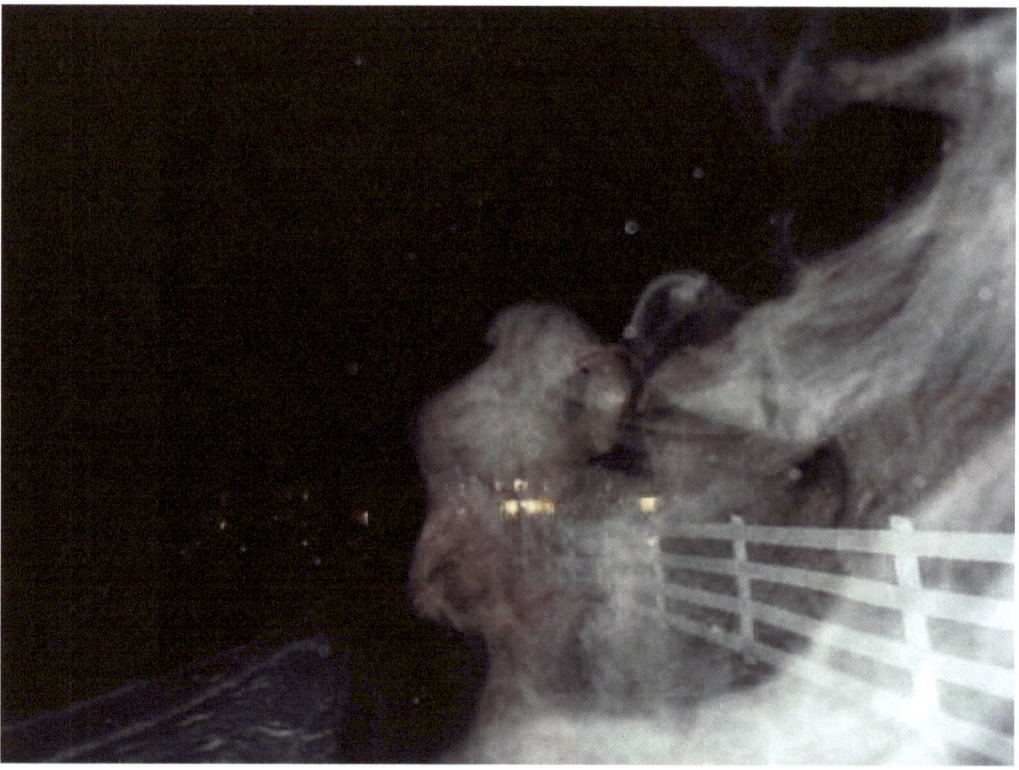

In the Myst-Art Gallery, the picture titled "Approaching Night" is described in the following way: "The evening lights of Mountain Quest form a conversational backdrop for reflecting on the lessons of the day." This is the picture featured on the cover of this book.

In more recent photographs taken with an 18.2-megapixel camera, there is greater clarity. The three pictures below are the same picture magnified. The top one presents as Dots and Circles, although at the upper right these Circles appear to be orbs (the second picture). The third picture takes a closer look. Can you see the faces? Repeated pictures of this nature lead us to ask: Is the center light in each Orb a face? If this is the case, it would seem that as the outer part of the Orb expands (using the water vapor in the air), the center part (which is brighter) retains the characteristics of a face. Is this how the faces are created in the *Myst*?

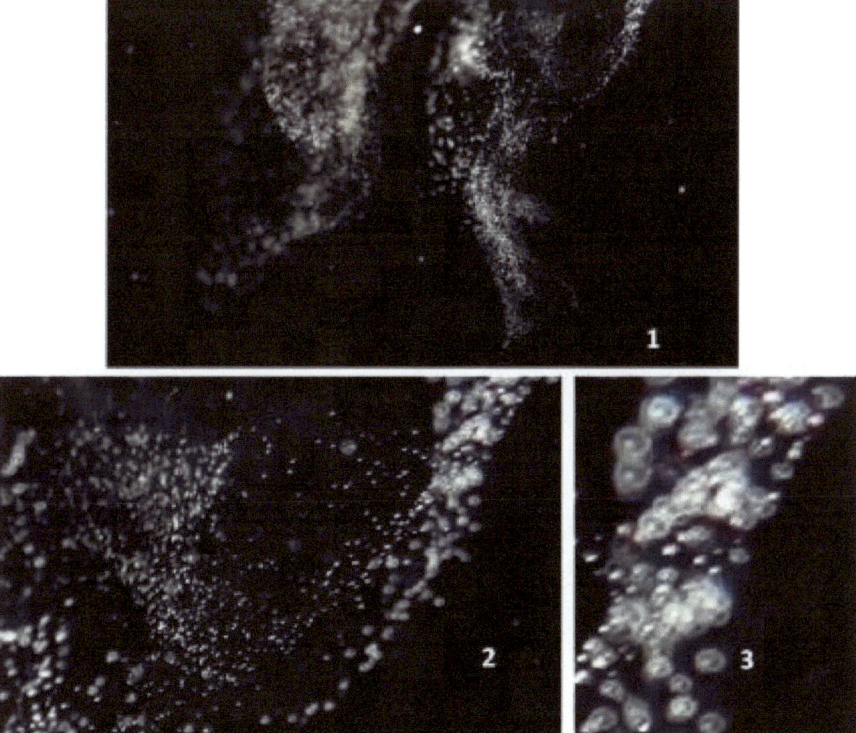

All of these pictures are from the same photograph, specifically, bringing the upper right of #1 into the clearer focus of #2, and even closer in #3. Below, we look even closer at the center of #3 in order to begin recognizing potential faces within the orbs. (Similar to page 22 in our earlier discussion).

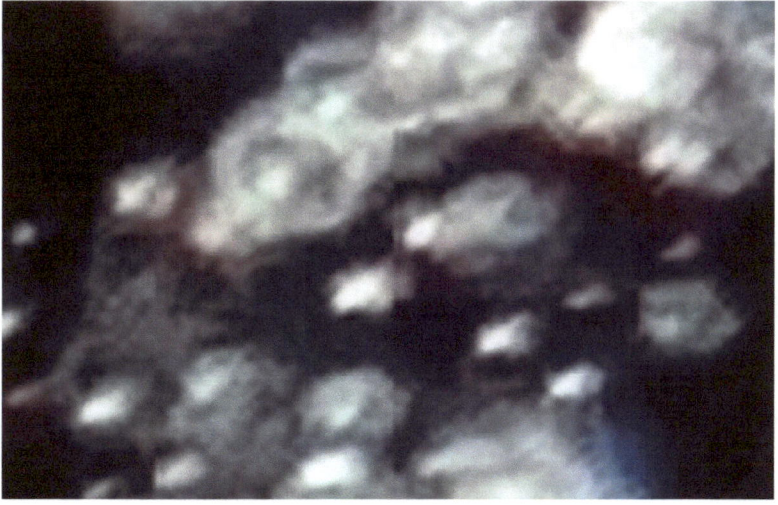

GUIDE CLOUDS

There are large numbers of photographs that appear to have groupings of faces in cloud-like *Myst*, sometimes on the outer edge, sometimes projecting from within the cloud itself. These *Myst* photographs are described as Guide Clouds. In the photograph below, if we look closely at one of the rounded/oval shapes that have two dark specks that are equal distance from the outside of the circle shape, and in the upper half of the shape, we perceive these as faces. A number of the 'faces" in this photograph have marks for mouths as well. The texture of this particular photograph is Cloud; most Guide Clouds (but not all!) have this texturing. Periodically a Guide Cloud will show aspects of Circles, and a larger number move into the Fluff texture. However, the name "Guide Clouds" is still used for these shapes with faces.

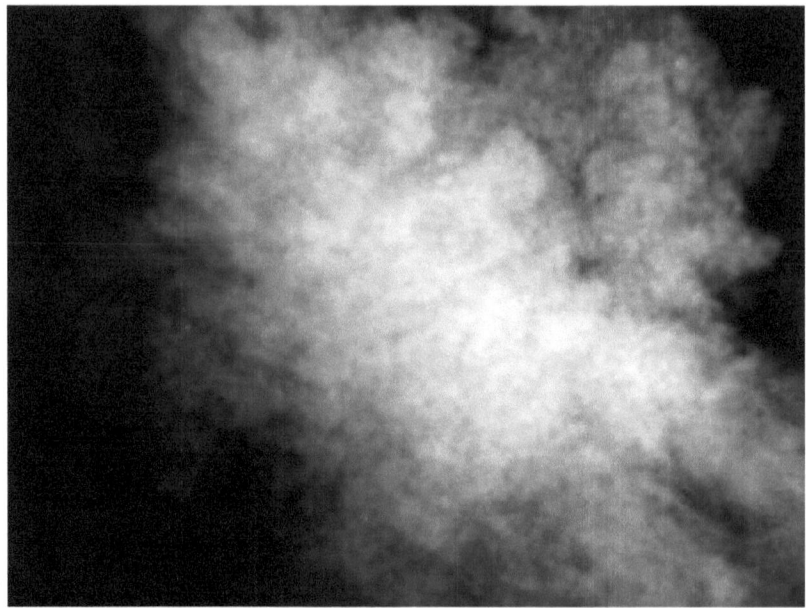

(Above) This Guide Cloud displays soft faces on the upper edge (Cloud texture). (Below) Another example of a Guide Cloud (Fluff texture).

Setting aside partial pictures, whiffs of *Myst* and unrecognizable shapes, the largest number of pictures that insinuate some recognizable pattern are of Guide Clouds, which present with multiple heads and faces (including animal heads and faces) generally around the edges. This may insinuate that there is some level of energy conservation in presenting collectively. The question becomes the source of the thicker parts of the Guide Clouds, the Cloud or Fluff textured shape that provides a foundation of sorts from which the heads and faces present. This core represents the largest energy outlay in the picture.

There's more to think about. Following this train of thought further, could it be that the *Myst* forms, and shapes where heads and faces are NOT visibly, present with less energy? There is also the timing of the camera flash to consider. As the battery begins to die the time between photographs increases. Further, the photographer's finger on the button can easily slip and shift the rhythm, causing an uneven pattern of flashes. So how can a Guide Cloud be perfectly formed at the exact instant of the flash?

Another consideration is that the *Myst* is emergent, and may be the thought projection of different groupings of orbs at different times or different places (acknowledging that time and space may not be as we perceive them). When asking Yes and No questions for external validation of the intelligence and responsiveness of the *Myst*, Alex noted that there were times when she felt the need to repeat the introduction to the process, after which there was more fluid interaction. This might denote different groups of *Myst* visitors.

All this by way of saying that, when the picture is captured, the *Myst* may or may not be in its highest energetic form. This might certainly affect the texture or form completeness of a specific photograph. On the other hand, this whole conversation was based on our perception of time.

For sake of discussion, let's bring one more point into the mix. There are nights when only circles occur, and other nights where almost every shot produces Fluff. The Fluff shots are more rare, especially those imbued with pink. The times when they occurred for a stretch of time were only after several hundred pictures had already been taken in the same area. It could be assumed that the flash was assisting in **priming the area for the appearance of higher energy *Myst* figures.** The Dots are even more rare, although variations in the environment (specifically, snow) seem to host more pictures of Dots.

Quite differently, the Bright Light figures, also rare, pop in for several shots at any time in the sequence. The only noted characteristic consistent with the appearance of Bright Light *Myst* is Alex's energy. These pictures always occurred when she was strongly feeling her oneness with the Universe and having such a welling of love inside that it often brought her to tears.

The Guide Cloud photograph below was taken early in the morning before the sun arose. Within the left part of the *Myst* Cloud is a section of Bright Light which has a faint hint of pink.

(Right) In the Myst-Art Gallery this photograph is titled "Coming of Day" and is described in this way: "Cloud guides absorbing knowledge of our dimension."

RIDERS OF THE *MYST*

Quite often there is the perception of a single form perched above or on other forms that appear to be moving in one direction or another. For example, in the photograph below there appears to be a *Myst* form (possibly Elemental energy) atop another form moving to the right, all this atop a farm cat that is preening himself! The rider has two marks for eyes and there is even a shadowing where a nose would be and a line where the mouth would be, although the mouth crosses the jaw line much like that of an animal, and the ears flop from the upper right, also more animal-like than human. The lower form (or forms) have pointed faces shaped somewhat like a triangle with enough pock marks to discover an eye if the viewer chooses to look for this. The texture is primarily Cloud with a hint of Circles near the top part of the rider. The stretched form of both the rider and that which is ridden as well as a brighter shape closer to the front of the picture conveys the feeling of movement to the right.

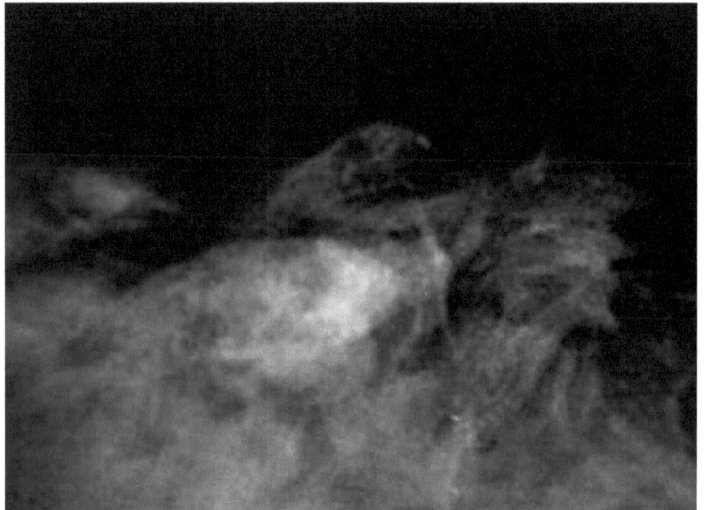 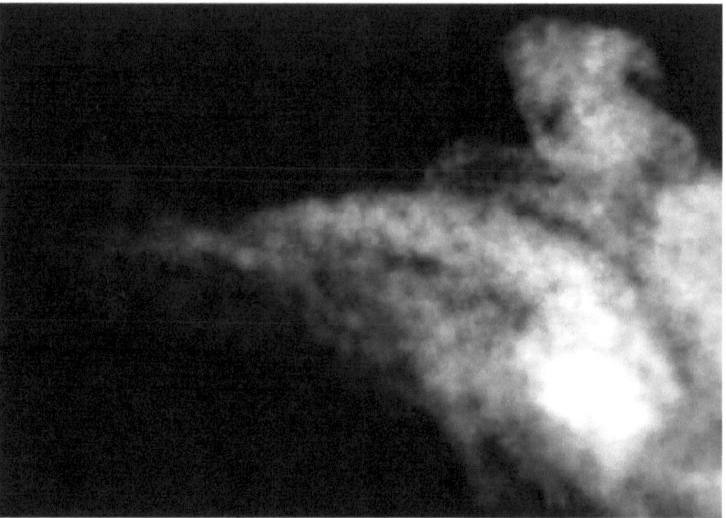

(Left) These stretched energy forms rising from the ground convey movement to the right. (Right) In the Myst-Art Gallery this picture is titled Dolphin Rider. The description is as follows: A Mysty form surfs the night sky riding the waves of expectation."

As we continue to explore the concept of a "rider", we move to what appears to be a dolphin and its rider (see the picture below). The dolphin's head is nicely formed with a large eye where it would be perceived. The figure atop appears to have a scarf or hood falling back off the head from the movement forward, but the arms are firmly planted on the top of the dolphin. The slant of the back is that of a rider, and the legs appear to be wrapped down over the side to some extent, although only a part of this was captured in the picture. Both *Myst* shapes are Circles with a softening to Cloud at the lower right of the picture just below a splash of Bright Light. The human-like rider has a larger degree of pink mixed through the Circle texturing and a dark demarcation shadow where visually the rider ends and the dolphin begins. There is also a hint of blue-green coloring in both the top of the dolphin and the front part of the rider. Again, the stretching and leaning toward the left gives the allusion of a flowing movement, this time to the left.

A third example is the picture that carries the name "*Myst* Rider" (see below), a picture that is near and dear to Alex. While this is clearly a Cloud texture, billowing at the top, it is punctuated with small circles of light. The figure riding the rolls of *Myst* stretching up to the left is a young woman, thin at the waist, filling out to the shoulder, with both arms held down and a bit back as if conveying pure joy in the moment. The head is tilted back from the body. The happy smile on the face confirms the feeling of joy. The eye marks, hairline and hair are discernible.

Alex's joy in this photo is her perceived feeling, later confirmed in her process of interacting with the *Myst* (see the first book in this series), that this rider is a young version of her older sister who passed a number of years before the photograph was taken.

(Right) This "Myst Rider" is described in the Myst-Art Gallery as follows: "A young figure joyfully rides rolls of Myst toward the eaves of the old farm house."

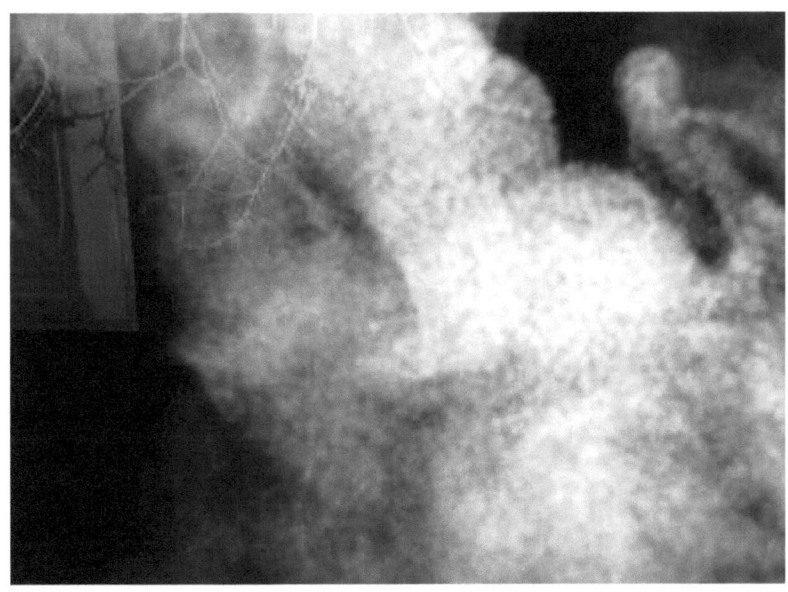

While an additional *Myst* rider photograph is featured in Chapter 6 in the discussion of interpretation and meaning, there is one additional rider that needs to be shared here because of the energy the figure exudes. This rider is actually engulfed in a large, gently curled *Myst* "hand" cloud, with her arms outstretched in front of her, hands connecting with the billowing *Myst*. The nose is distinct, the eyes are large, and a swath of hair blows out behind her, combining with the tilt of her arms to provide the allusion of a lifting up and movement to the left. Several viewers identify this as a golfer, which indeed it may be. The texture is Cloud, again with some circle accents, particularly to the right of the *Myst* hand, and there are some gentle splashes of Bright Light closer to the center of the picture.

This chapter moved from presentation of pictures representing Elemental Energy to Faces to Guide Clouds to figures riding the *Myst*. Through this process we have used the descriptive approaches developed in the earlier chapters to try and differentiate the *Myst* pictures. However, this is not enough. As can be seen in the discussions above, the "feelings" and "perceptions" of the authors began to creep into the descriptive passages. It is time to focus on building a deeper understanding of interpretation and meaning.

(Right) This photograph is titled "On the Rise" in and is described in this way: A young figure ascending the Myst in her quest for knowledge, consciousness and meaning." The three focus areas of Mountain Quest research are the search for knowledge, consciousness and meaning.

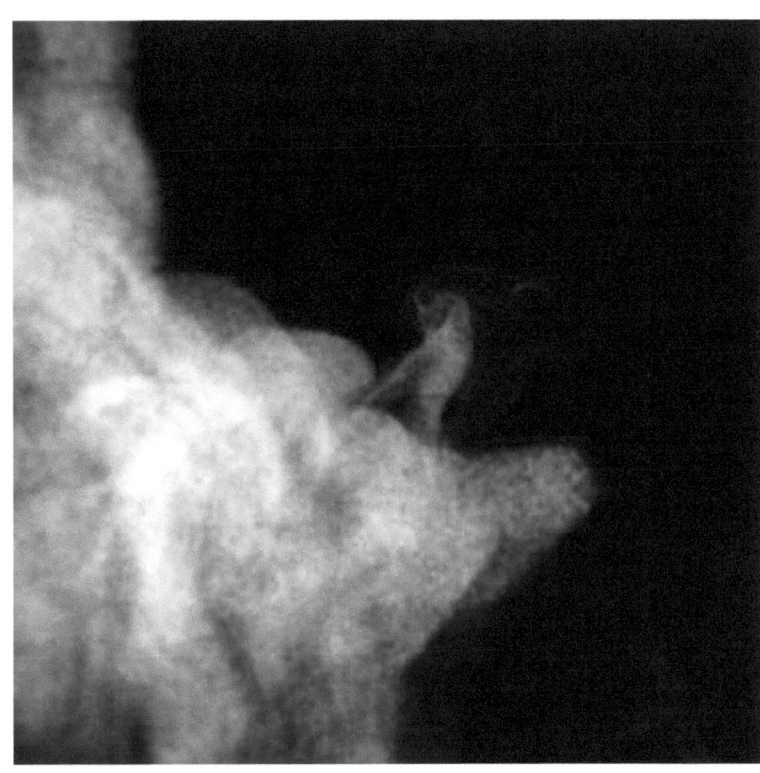

Chapter 6: Interpretation and Meaning

Consistent with the opening remarks in Chapter 1 and the further explanation in Endnote 1, information is considered as any non-random pattern. It may or may not have meaning, depending on one's ability to interpret and understand the patterns. For example, if the patterns were in Chinese symbols then they would be meaningless to anyone who did not know Chinese.

We define knowledge as the capacity (potential or actual) to take effective action. To understand this definition, it is necessary to understand the mind/brain, which is an associative patterner. Incoming information that comes through any of the senses is complexed (or associated) with relevant information that has been stored within the brain in the form of neuronal connection patterns and their synaptic strengths, and then may be "recreated" in a new way for the moment at hand. The mind is usually considering the current situation and then anticipating the outcome of its actions. To make this easier to understand, it is convenient to think about knowledge in terms of knowledge (informing) and knowledge (proceeding). Knowledge (informing) is the information part of knowledge, that is, all of the information coming into the mind/brain or that is being pulled up into consciousness from the unconscious. This would include our values and belief systems, and is consistent with the philosophical definition of knowledge as justified true belief. Knowledge (proceeding) is the process part of knowledge, the way each of us connects and integrates (associates) the information (patterns of neurons and their connections) in order to know how to actually take effective action in a particular situation. (Bennet and Bennet, 2008c)

Knowledge is a human capacity to comprehend and successfully navigate life, and may be composed of awareness, understanding, meaning, insight, intuition, creativity, judgment, and anticipating the future. While our focus in this chapter is on interpretation and meaning, neither of those can consciously occur without first building awareness, which was the intent of the first volume in the MQI *Myst* Series, *The Journey into the Myst*. Building awareness and some level of understanding has been supported in the earlier parts of this book. This process continues as we move into meaning-making.

One way to perceive and understand the invisible forces that produce *Myst*-Art is by their effects (Abrams and Primack, 2011). Effects include:

Visible produce (scene, picture)

Feelings (emotion, connection, love and joy)

Intuitive (How it can remind a conscious mind of things in memory and experience in the unconscious. The mind "feels" it is something more; and we are reminded of something "nice, beautiful, exciting." An example of this is: I really like that picture but I don't know why. Intuitive feeling may provide one meaning of the patterns.)

Logical (Matching patterns to previously known patterns, discovery of new patterns. An example is seeing faces in the *Myst*.)

Spiritual (invisible within, seeing is believing)

Evolution (A shift in thinking, a picture triggering something back in the early history of humanity, a feeling of evolution, even back to the stars from whence we came.)

Embodied (How the body reacts, the dancing and singing, smiling, the heartbeat, engagement with the brain/mind/body.)

* * * * *

Susan:

Seeing is believing! This work is evolutionary, showing me something that I could only imagine, and showing it in a consistent way. The *Myst* appears over here and over there, and I see patterns. It has evolved from something only in my imagination to something I can see.

* * * * *

MEANING

Meaning is taking information and determining the impact that information could have on you and your actions. We live in an illusion of separateness, and from each of our unique viewpoints (as subject) we observe other people and things (as objects) as we engage in living our day-to-day lives.

Meaning is highly individualized and provides the effect or impact of what something is to "Me," that is, based very much on individual beliefs and experiences engaged both consciously and unconsciously. From the perspective of our personal viewpoint, we tend to see what we are looking for. In addition to our belief system, our interests and current state of feelings directly impact our interpretation of the world around us. When we consider the fact that we all live within our personal self-created illusion of the external world, we recognize that what we see in a picture is viewed within the narrow bounds of our personal illusion of what is or is not "real". For example, when we are standing or sitting down, we think that we are not moving, but in fact we are moving at 67,000 miles per hour as the earth hurtles around the Sun.

The Dihedral Group Theory[6] approach to meaning-making helps individuals understand their personal focus, that is, where their awareness is centered. For example, take the simple statement "Alex captured *Myst* pictures." If Alex is ego-centric, then the focus will be the subject of the sentence, Alex, and the capture process and *Myst* pictures will reflect her personal viewpoints. If Alex is process-centric, then the *capture* will be the focus, and who is capturing and what is being captured will be a subset of the process itself. If Alex is empathetic, then the *Myst* is the focus, and the photographer and process are just facilitators of the *Myst* pictures. All three are legitimate ways of meaning-making. The Dihedral Group Theory approach asks you to shift your frames of reference to six different models, each changing the relationship of subject/verb/object. Shifting Frames of Reference is a Knowledge Capacity.[7]

Myst-Art pictures are information until the viewer connects some *Myst* pattern with something that is historically familiar or internally felt or believed. When exploring a pattern or set of patterns, there may be insufficient experience to identify meaning. It may be necessary to take the information at hand and create some new knowledge, understanding and insight about it. *Ask:* Do we have sufficient knowledge about the information (pattern) to actually create and interpret its meaning. One way to do this is to explore the surrounding context. This is why we began the first book in this series with the story of a miracle, which helps explain the frame of reference shift that supported the authors exploring this phenomenon from a spiritual perspective as well as a physical perspective. The story oriented the reader to the mystical. Think about the symbolism of a miracle, what it says to you, what it says about human life. *Ask:* What part of the story stands out most strongly? Why might that be the most important to you? These "feelings" contribute to our meaning-making of the events that followed the miracle.

One approach to meaning-making is to start with the end in mind. *Ask:* What are we trying to do; what do we want to see; what do we want to come out of our interpretation? What qualities of the *Myst* are we looking for in terms of shape and texture? Why might these be important?

Another starting point is to ask what we think and how we feel about a specific picture. *Ask:* What is my reaction to the picture (emotional, intuitive, mental, spiritual)? What does this photograph say to me? Does it relate to something in which I am involved? Could it impact something in which I am interested? What could be potentially learned from this phenomenon? What knowledge can I create from this photograph? How does this knowledge relate to me personally? What can/should I do with this knowledge?

And finally, think in terms of action. *Ask:* Is the *Myst* figure doing anything? Is there a specific action in which the *Myst* figure appears to be engaged? What state of that action does the picture capture? Does this photograph suggest any actions that I should take?

When exploring a pattern in the *Myst*, the pattern would have meaning in terms of what's causing it, how we interpret it, the situation and context, and how we can interpret and comprehend the pattern based on our own experience and knowledge. For example, the authors are always asking questions about the relationship between the *Myst* images and reality. After drawing on personal resources and dialogue among the two of them, they seek additional viewpoints, drawing on other people as resources and experts with different experiences and insights. Friends, colleagues and guests of the Mountain Quest Institute have all contributed to our current understanding.

Each *Myst*-Art picture contains a number of patterns which may be interpretable by the viewer. When we begin to associate one aspect of a *Myst* form to something familiar, other aspects begin to emerge. This is the associative patterning part of the human mind/brain (see Endnote 2). One familiar thought or part of a thought connects with a network of neuronal firings and now there is a focus to identify those things in the *Myst* that might represent the thing triggered in the mind/brain, and so forth. In other words, we must find the first trigger. Then, once the first trigger occurs, there is little that is objective. The exercise of associating is highly subjective, and the meaning of the *Myst*, like knowledge, is context sensitive and situation dependent. The meaning of any picture may easily be different for different observers. Meaning is created in the mind of the observer!

Both the conscious "me" and my unconscious interact with the external world. For example, when driving a car, the driver is often talking and/or thinking about something entirely different (conscious focus), yet the driver's unconscious ensures that the car moves "automatically" and safely along. If an emergency arises in the midst of a conversation, conscious attention is immediately drawn to that emergency. Through this simple example it is clear that the unconscious has a role to play in relating to the external world. As Mlodinow (2012) so clearly demonstrates in what he calls the "fluency effect", our unconscious mind plays a much larger role in our lives than previously thought.

When interpreting a *Myst* picture, both the conscious and unconscious have a role to play. For example, when asking the question "How do you feel about this picture?" the emotions are being used as an indicator of the unconscious processing of meaning. Emotions play an important role in this probing of nature. Here is how two guests at Mountain Quest, both of whom were able to get *Myst* pictures, interpreted their experience.

* * * * *

Bob and Jane:

What is this amazing new communion with nature? As accounts of orbs from around the world become pervasive, there are increasing glimpses of concurrent mist activity. Now, at Mountain Quest Institute and Inn in West Virginia, the mist phenomenon is being experienced at a breakthrough point. The quality of this

Mountain Quest experience with mists is another remarkable interaction with nature in this idyllic setting. Mountain Quest is a rural destination that presents in an almost hidden mountain glen—a beautiful lush valley at an elevation of 2,585 feet with a cresting mountain for a backdrop. This is a serene and nearly surreal environment that opens up your senses ...

Indeed, the mists at Mountain Quest engender more than observation—there is a sense of communication, a two-way process that offers participation. As with contemplation and meditation, there is invitation to reach beyond one's normal awareness to appreciate and imagine—to discover. Initially the mists appear in a quiet whimsical way—they frolic in fanciful and fun shapes. Then, profuse patterns, images, scenes, movements, and even colors emerge. As you carefully explore, your imagination soars and the drama unfolds.

What is the scientific relationship between the orbs and the mists? What drives the density? Digital photography easily enables you to capture hundreds and thousands of complex images, but what are you missing? If you are seeing the essence of the images, what do they represent? When you watch cloud formations, your mind quickly deciphers whimsical scenes. You perceive, then you imagine. With the mist, it seems as if nature comes up to create for you, then you perceive and interpret. When you observe the mist, it's like you are witnessing provocative emissaries from nature. There is depth in the scenes that resonates—it's like nature conversing with you on an intimate level. You perceive visually and you interpret from your own experience with enough vividness that you want to share your perceptions.

Just a short jaunt from Mountain Quest, there's more than a modicum of irony in the existence of another reach beyond. Up the road is the site of the National Radio Astronomy Observatory, a research project of the National Science Foundation. While NRAO probes space with a 17 million pound, 100-meter wide, single dish radio telescope, Mountain Quest probes nature with a handheld digital camera.

* * * * *

Bob and Jane added context to their experience with the *Myst* by juxtaposing the exploration of the Cosmos occurring at the National Radio Astronomy Observatory (just down the road) with the exploration of the *Myst* energies at Mountain Quest. This juxtaposing starts surfacing assumptions and raises additional questions.

Another part of context is the background setting. For example, many of the photographs in the *Myst*-Art Gallery are taken in front of mountains. Throughout history mountains have symbolized power and a loftiness of spirit, linking heaven and Earth. To the Chinese mountains are symbolic of generosity and greatness, often symbolizing dragons. Mountains exude a masculine energy. In contrast, forests are connected to creation and birth, places where vegetation and animals thrive. This feminine energy is symbolic of freedom, creative forces and the loosening of the unconscious, another appropriate background for *Myst* pictures (Andrews, 2005).

Direction from which the *Myst* appears may also be symbolic. Alex has noticed that there are evenings when the *Myst* continuously appears from one direction or the other, although this is not consistent from night to night. There are other evenings when Alex uses her red sensor light in combination with the camera flash to follow the movement of the *Myst* as it moves around her or over her. These differences may reflect the amount of available energy for the Myst to form and shape. There is some priming that occurs in the area where the flash of the camera appears, that is, the building of electromagnetic energy. On nights where the weather conditions are prime—noting that a higher level of water in the air and a lower temperature combine to accelerate the appearance of the *Myst*—the *Myst* moves freely, forming and shaping around

Alex. There are some occasions where this movement can also be directly related to the interaction between Alex and the Myst. For example, one night (as described earlier), Alex was wistfully looking at the stars above and stated out loud that she would like to see a shooting star. On this night the *Myst* moved, and as Alex turned to follow, she saw (at different times) three shooting stars!

MEANING UNFOLDING

Since the mind is an associative patterner, one idea has a tendency to lead to another and another. Such was the case with eagle beaks. In the two photographs below you will see the similarity between the face embedded below an Eagle's Head shaped hat and the sketch of an Eagle's Head Hat Mask (compliments of artist Cindy Taylor) used by Shamans in Indian ceremonies. [A Shaman is a priest or priestess in certain tribal societies who is the connection between the visible world and the invisible world.] These shapes appear periodically in the *Myst* pictures taken at Mountain Quest, across which a Cherokee hunting trail winds. Indian arrowheads are often found when the fields are turned for planting.

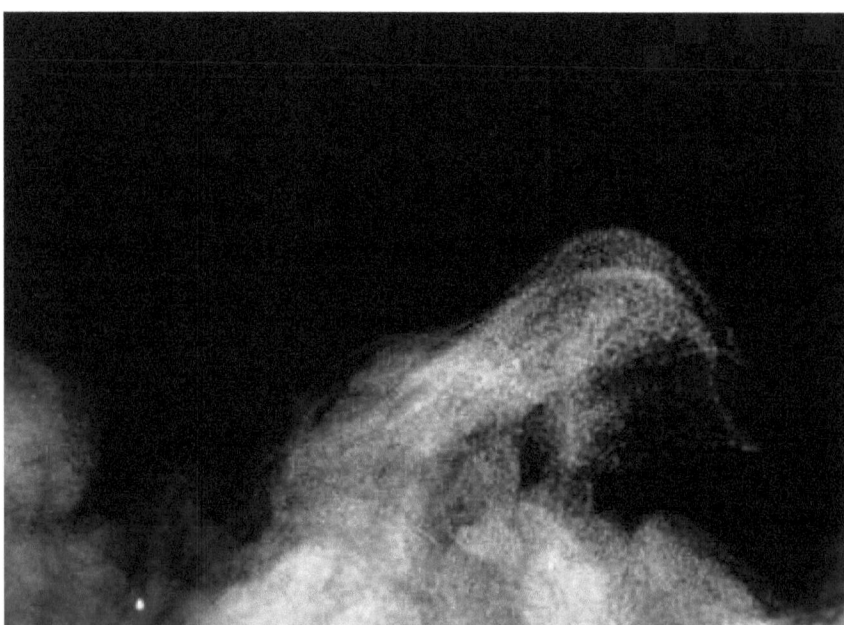

(Left) An example of "beaks" with a face beneath, representing a Shaman most likely of the Cherokee tribe. A Cherokee hunting trail runs across Mountain Quest. (Below) This is an artist's sketch of a Shaman in an eagle's beak mask.

Relating these forms to Indian rituals expands thinking by considering other *Myst* forms that may relate to Indians. For example, when a Cherokee descendant was at Mountain Quest doing research for her Ph.D. studies, she was able to point out other *Myst* pictures representing Native American energies. In the photograph on the next page, the left pink swirls represent an Indian warrior riding his horse in the Myst. These are the guardians of the land. This photograph presents in Fluff with several colors of high-energy pink throughout.

When Alex first saw this photograph, she perceived the figure as a Cherub, but once the horse form was pointed out to her, she was excited to see another Native American picture. The Mountain Quest farm, situated on 450 acres in a high valley of the Allegheny Mountains, has offered hundreds of arrowheads when the upper fields were deep plowed. As the story goes, the farm is part of former Cherokee Hunting Grounds and the upper field served as a camp site.

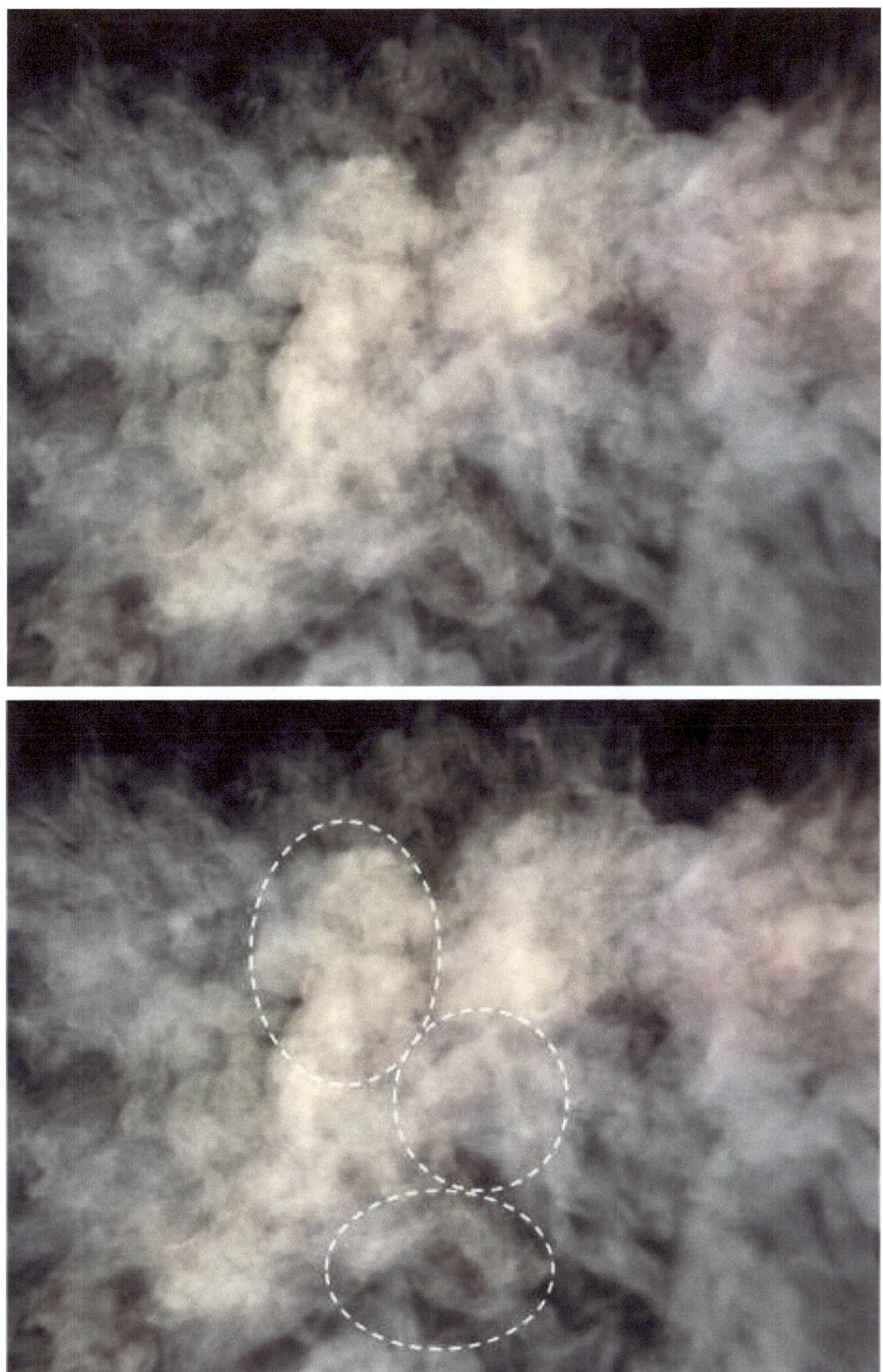

(Top) This picture is titled "Energy Burst" in the Myst-Art Gallery with the description: The guardians of Mountain Quest riding the Myst. (Above) The dotted lines circle the Indian rider's upper body and the horse's head and right front leg.

ANIMALS

Myst shapes can often be interpreted as specific animals. For example, Alex has on multiple occasions captured images that look like a giraffe or an elephant.

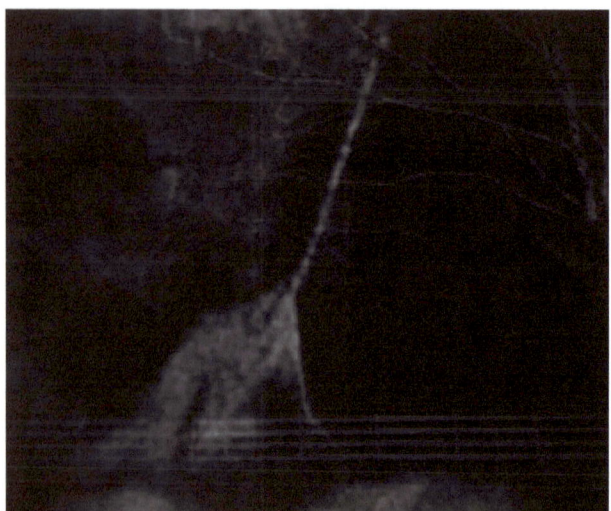 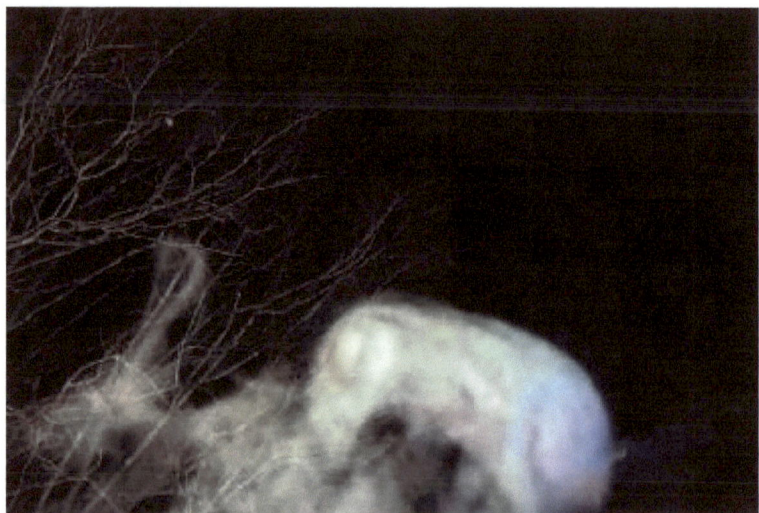

(Left) Walking out the front door with camera in hand, Alex is greeted by a giraffe with his head in the Maple tree. (Right) Some friendly Myst animals present in the front yard.

Referring to *Animal Speak: The Spiritual & Magical Powers of Animals Great and Small* (Andrews, 2005), the long neck of the giraffe is symbolic of foreseeing events to come, a bridging to cross over into new realms and new perceptions. The long legs represent balance and the ability to progress with your feet on the ground and head in the sky. The lump in the center of the forehead is associated with the third eye, the seat of higher intuition. Digging more deeply into these representations can help the viewer understand potential messages. For example, the appearance of a giraffe in the *Myst* first occurred when Alex and David were trying to decide how to move forward with sharing what they were learning about the *Myst*, how far to openly talk about the *Myst* and their expanding Spiritual beliefs. Both Alex and David are respected professionals in their area of study around knowledge and learning.

The elephant is connected to the dreams of great teachers and masters. It is associated with strength and power, and well as wisdom and success, and faithfulness and intellect. As with our dreams, the specific interpretation is very individualized, that is, ask yourself what does it represent to me? It also depends on what the elephant you see if doing. For example, if the elephant is eating it may mean you are going to receive some money.

Similarly, pay attention to the color. If the elephant is white, as is our example, it may bring good fortune, or even reflect a spiritual goodness. The Animal Speak book referenced in the previous paragraph, is an excellent text for exploring the meanings of various animals. It begins on the foundation that we are a part of nature, always connected to the Earth and it to us. Animal Speak refers to a time when animals and humans were able to speak with each other, sometimes by animals learning our language, and other times by us learning the language of animals. The *Myst* is part of this natural world and appears to take on the form of animals quite often. On the other hand, we must ask: could this be partly because we are a farm? But then, the forms of animals we've been exploring were not farm animals. However, animals that become closer parts of human life also present.

Symbolically, dogs reflect faithfulness and protection. For both Alex and David, the appearance of dog shapes and faces in the *Myst* held deep meaning. In *The Journey into the Myst* Alex shared the wonderful story of Kumo's appearance in the *Myst* following his difficult transition. The two beautiful Fluff photographs featured with that story greatly strengthened Alex's connections with the *Myst*. One of these photographs is shown below. Behind the beautiful *Myst* interspersed with the pink Fluff that is Kumo (with his back legs presenting as wings), is a dark face echoing Sashi (Kumo's older sister who passed a year earlier than Kumo).

*This beautiful Fluff photograph is entitled "Friends of Light" in the Myst-Art Gallery.
It is featured in the first book of this series, The Journey into the Light.*

Perhaps because she looks for them, Alex often notices the features of Kumo and/or Sashi in the *Myst*. What she found surprising was that a visitor to the Inn who she took out to try and capture *Myst* pictures was able to get a clear picture of Sashi! The first photograph on the next page (to the left) was taken by Margie Schaeffer (a visitor at the Inn) on October 8, 2011. For comparison purposes, the second picture is Sashi taken in 2009 prior to her death.

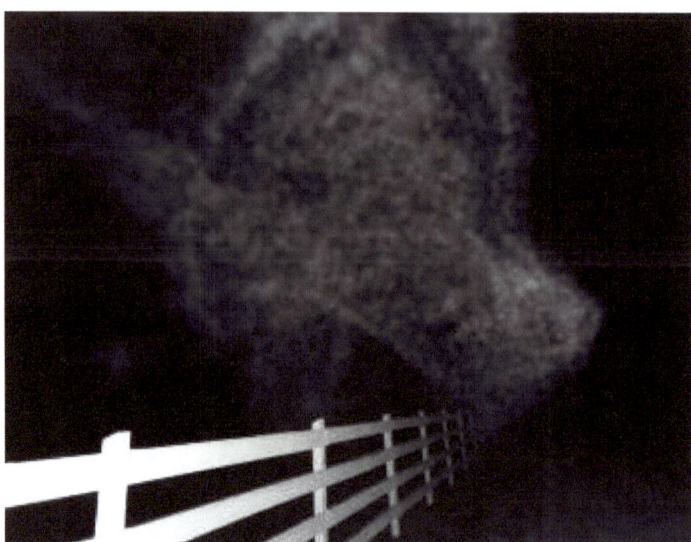 

Explore the similarity in the faces of these pictures. (Left) The Myst picture becomes clearer when compared to the second one, a picture of Sashi before she passed as she greets Zebo, a feral friend to many visitors of the Mountain Quest Inn.

Because of her experience with Kumo after his passing, when Alex and David's 30-year-old Arabian mare Zatara passed in the Spring of 2011, Alex was expecting her appearance in the *Myst*. She wasn't disappointed. Alex called upon her angels and guides to bring Zatara into the light and watch over her. Zatara had been the riding mare for children on many occasions. Particularly memorable was a horse-care experience held several years earlier for girls aged 8-13. As Alex sang her request for support of this beautiful animal's transition, she expressed the joy engendered in these young riders by Zatara. This was a life well-lived.

The first picture Alex caught of Zatara is magnificent, even though the camera didn't catch the front part of Zatara's face. In this remarkable photograph, the face of Zatara presents as small Circles or large Dots, while the mane is Dots with Fluff accents of Soft Light. There is a Light Striation at Zatara's chin. Dancing amidst her mane are Cloaked Visitors (discussed in Chapter 8).

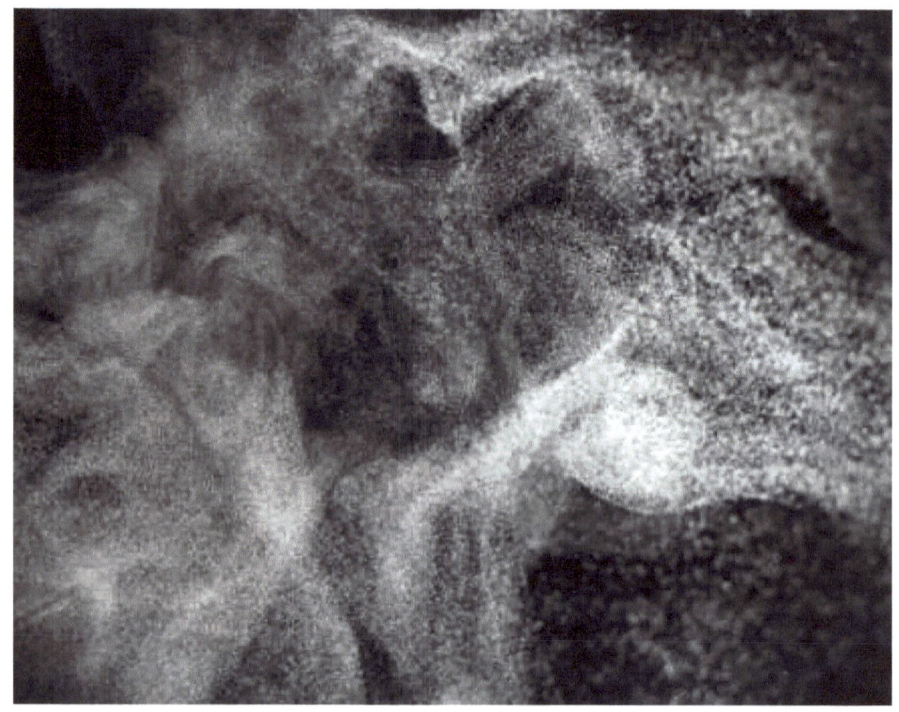

(Right) In the Gallery, this picture is titled "Ride the Wind" and is described as: The mane of the beautiful white Myst Arabian mare Zatara (translating "tumbleweed") explodes with cloaked faces.

Before Zatara passed, Alex cut her forelock as a keepsake to hold this beautiful mare in memory. Now seeing Zatara in the *Myst*, Alex asked if it was all right, if her forelock had grown back. That was when Alex took the picture of the *Myst* shown below to the left (textured Circles with accents of Dots). This picture took on great significance to Alex. Below to the right is the forelock that Alex cut off as a keepsake. As you can see, the resemblance is remarkable, and a welcome response to Alex. An isn't it interesting that the texturing of the Zatara as *Myst* in the photo below is similar to her presentation on the previous page?

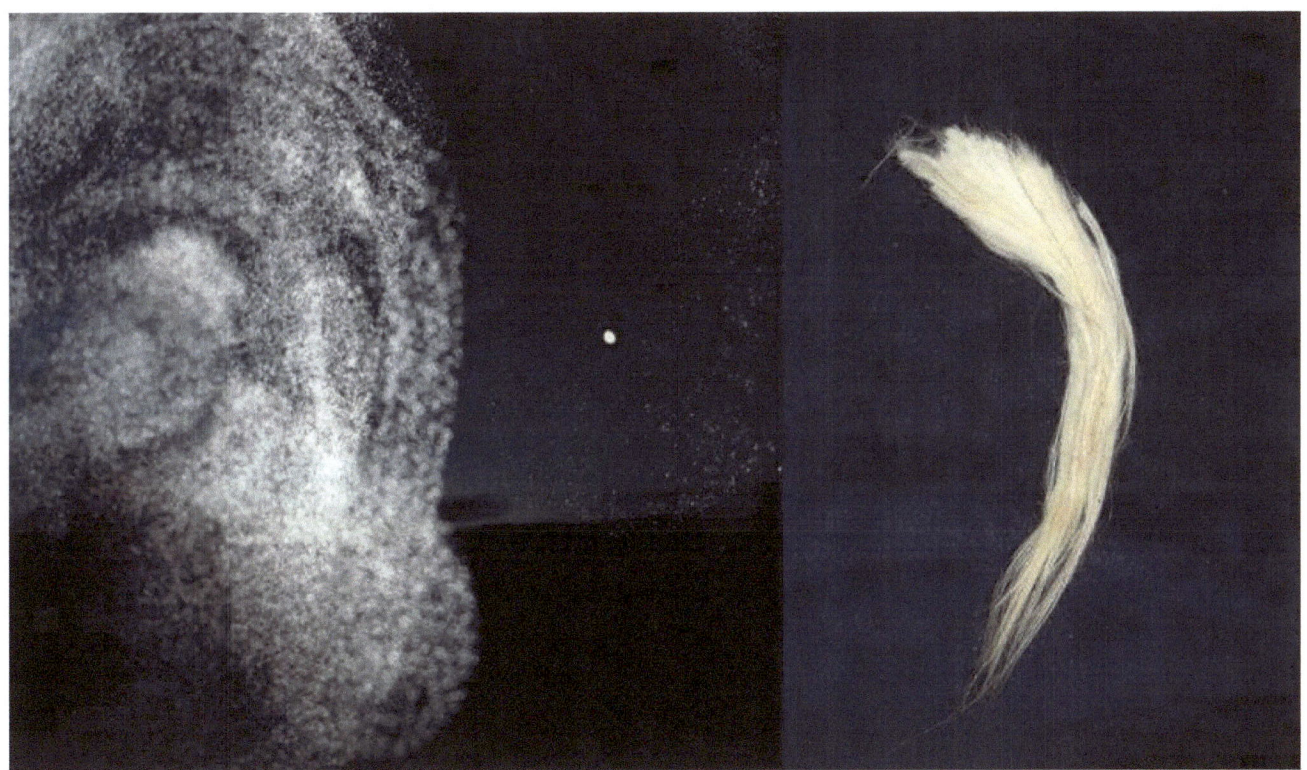

The picture to the right is the forelock Alex kept from Zatara. To the left is a picture of Zatara in the Myst with her full forelock accented. This photograph is titled "Zatara" in the Myst-Art collection and described as: "The beautiful Arabian Myst mare Zatara reminds us that life triumphs."

Horses appear in the *Myst* in many different poses and shapes. For example, in the photograph below a swooping shape dips down towards the barn and paddocks. The *Myst* is primarily Circles with several light striations. In the background is the 110-year-old farmhouse, making the direction of the appearance of this photograph to the South. One characteristic of "South" symbolism is playfulness.

(Right) This photograph is titled "Horse Play" in the Myst-Art Gallery and is described as: The amazing Myst forms a familiar shape as it swoops down towards the barn and paddocks.

As a footnote here, the *Myst* often appears around the physical horses at Mountain Quest, both inside and outside the barn as well as in the fields. Alex has spent many nights in the company of the horses just enjoying the interaction with the *Myst*.

 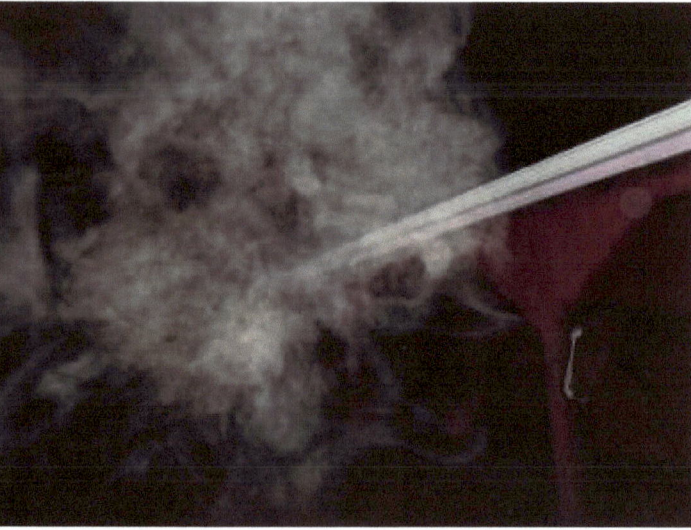

(Left) Alex's beautiful black Visuelle comfortable with the natural energy of the Myst. (Right) This photograph is entitled "Cracker's Dilemma" in the Gallery. What shapes can you perceive in the Myst?

JUXTAPOSING POSITIVE AND NEGATIVE ENERGIES

Since we have very much lived in a dualistic world (right/wrong, yes/no, winner/loser, etc.),[8] a serious consideration regarding the phenomenon of the *Myst* as well as the patterns viewed in each picture was the question regarding positive and negative energies. Let's address this issue at several levels.

Regarding the beginning of the phenomenon itself, as detailed in *The Journey into the Myst* Alex's immediate question upon seeing the first *Myst* character with her eyes (not just through the camera lens) was: "Should I be afraid?" The response was what Alex perceived as a hand touching her left shoulder and waves of love filling her body. In response, Alex acknowledged that anything projecting love held no fear for her. This resonance of love and joy is explored in Chapter 5.

However, the premise of higher order emotion that underlies Alex's participation in this phenomenon does not preclude the capture of some *Myst* figures that could be interpreted as representing negative energies. For example, below is a picture of a jackal who looks like he is attacking something on the ground.

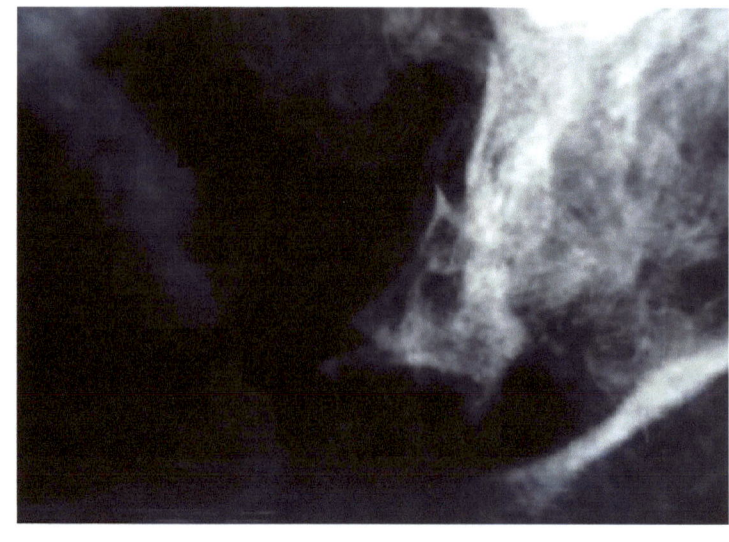

(Right) This photograph is titled "Wild Myst" in the Myst-Art Gallery and described as a mythological creature aggressively charging into the night.

This picture of a jackal presents as Cloud (although there is the hint of Circles in the Cloud and areas of Pocked) with strong light striations. This *Myst* figure exudes movement/action through extended characteristics of the open mouth and leg. What message could it convey? Jackals are scavengers and carrion eaters, giving rise to their association with death. The Egyptian god Anubis (with a jackal head) was believed to care for the immortal soul of the dead, bringing those souls to the Otherworld Judgment Hall, and returning the energy of the deceased to the life cycle. This can also represent the death of a particular way of being, portending a new birth. According to "The White Goddess" website on animal spirit guides, the jackal's wisdom includes: astral travel, accessing past lives, understanding the use of opportunity and the ability to see in the dark. the point that is made here is that even something that we perceive as negative has the possibility of messaging an important—and potentially positive—message.

In the photograph below, one interpretation might be that of an animal who has cornered its prey. This photograph presents primarily as Pocked. Note the distinctiveness of the eye, ears and open mouth.

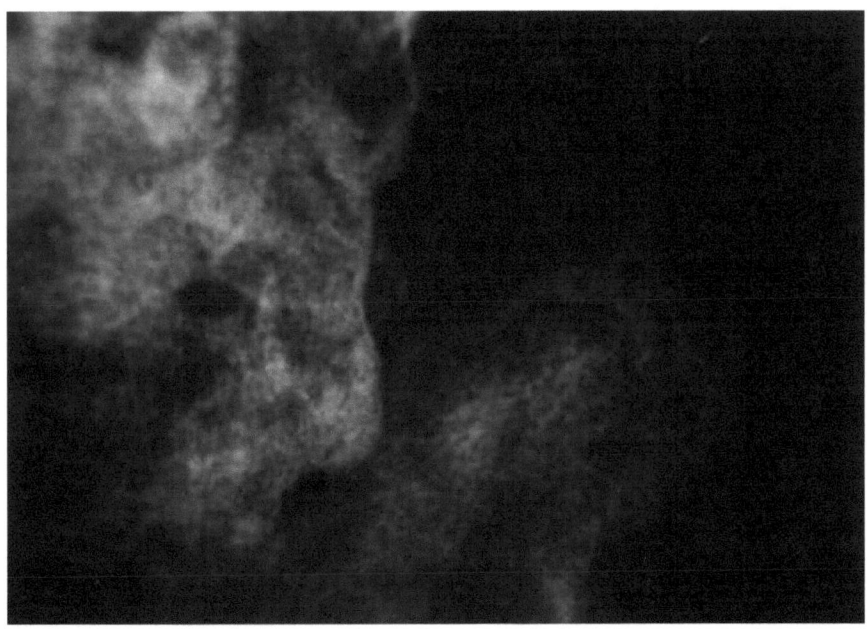

(Above) This photograph is titled "The Capture" and described as a Myst hunter approaching small wisps of light in the dark sky.

In *Animal Speak*, a comprehensive dictionary of animal, bird and reptile symbolism, Ted Andrews' reminds us that nature constantly speaks through its shapes, colors, textures, smells and varied expressions of animal life. The symbolism of Nature varies according to its context, so in order to understand that symbolism we must understand the natural context. Just as ancient augurs studied Nature, we are encouraged to reopen the lines of communication to send and receive messages from the Universe. (Andrews, 2005)

In one chapter dedicated to "The Mystery and Magic of Predator and Prey", Andrews describes the predatory process (predation) as taking time, patience and skill that sharpens the senses with the strongest, most alert and knowledgeable animals surviving. Animals grow stronger and wiser trying to avoid being caught. The detailed lessons that are part of the predation process deal with life, death and rebirth (creation); adaptation (shapeshifting); using your potential (manifestation); and responsible relationships (higher vision and prophecy). Finally, Andrews (2005) points out that there is a universality and balance found within the mysteries of predation in the natural world that can be ours if we learn to work them. In the context of "symbolism" and with the brief discussion above of the predation process, what meaning might be found in the above picture?

The representation of potentially positive and negative energies is not restricted to the animal kingdom. One dramatic example is the photograph below entitled "Drama in the Night" which depicts a Council in the *Myst* observing the struggle between good and evil. We see the back of the figure to the lower left who appears to be holding a sickle attacking another figure to his right (and less distinct) who is holding a similar weapon in his hand. In the upper part of the picture (to the left but swooping in from the right) is a watching face. The picture primarily presents as Cloud with Fluff accenting the lower left figure, and light striations helping to form and shape the figures appearing in the rest of the picture. This scene could easily represent the warring nature of three-dimensional man, a scene that with the shift of Earth and Human energies birthed in December 2012 will soon lose its representative nature.

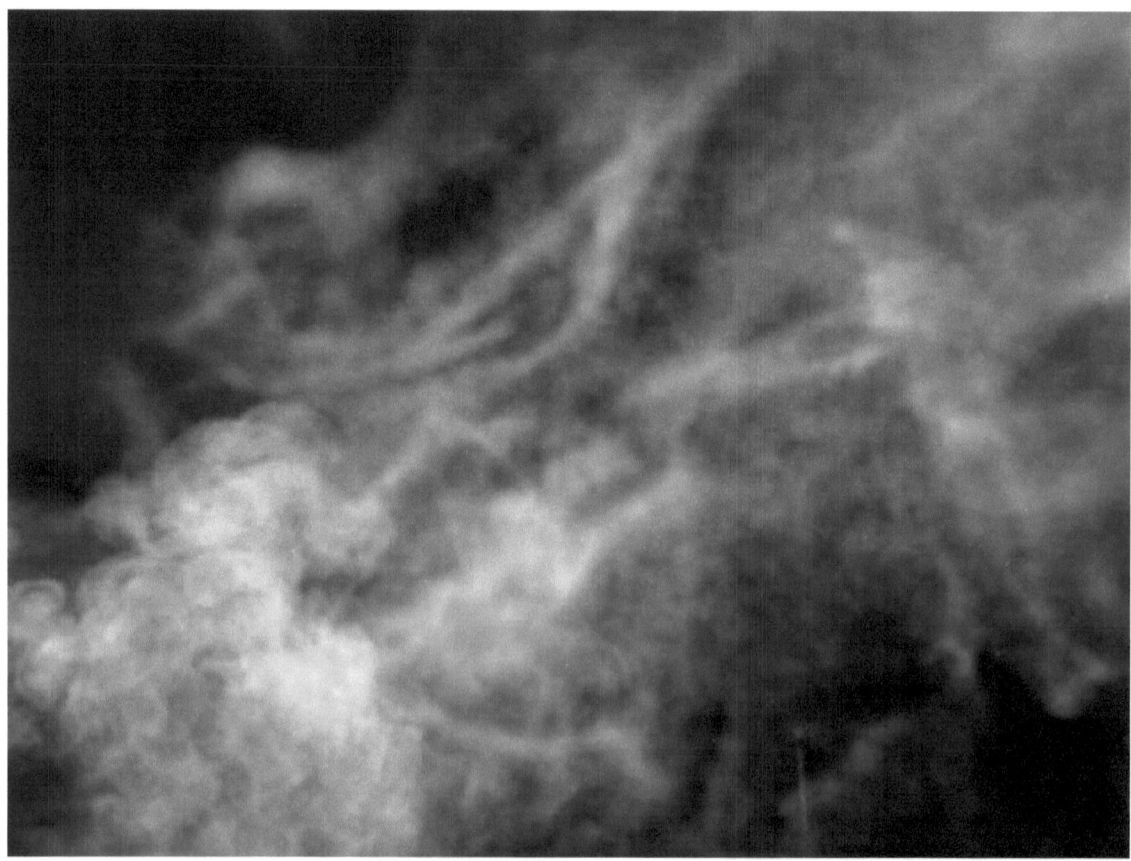

(Above) This picture is titled "Drama in the Night" in the Myst-Art Gallery and described as a depiction of the Council in the Myst observing the struggle between good and evil.

As one last example, in the picture below there is the appearance of some large creature (a dragon?) looming over two women whose faces are raised upwards toward the creature. The two women have shawls over their heads representing an earlier time in history. The first impression is that of fear, forwarding the idea that the two women are fleeing from an attack.

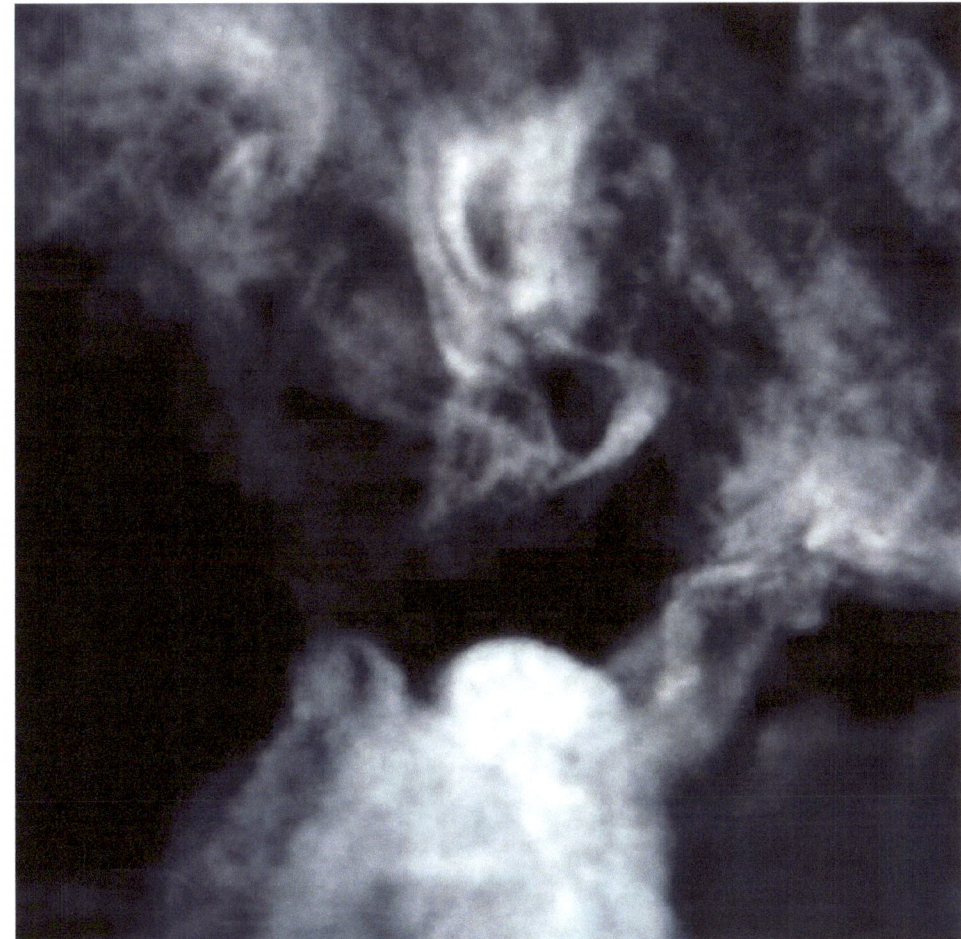

This picture, which we explored earlier in another context, is titled "Look to the Skies" with the following description: Fear? Look beyond the first impression to the essence of actuality.

Upon closer observation, it appears there are a number of faces that present from the upper Cloud and Fluff formation. For example, to the left of the "dragon" head (presented in light striations) a smiling face is peering down towards the women. Further, while very bright and less defined, the face of the woman to the right conveys the feeling of dismay or fear. Yet the face of the woman to the left (more defined) conveys the idea of interest and reflection. Again, we are called to reexamine our first premise of a historic representation of two women fleeing from an attack and reflect on other possibilities.

Chapter 7: Taking a Closer Look

There are many pictures that are so intriguing that Alex and David keep returning to them to reflect on their beauty and meaning. A few of these are discussed below, with particular focus on the "feelings" the pictures engender in the authors.

WHAT DOES GOD LOOK LIKE?

The photograph in the *Myst*-Art Gallery entitled "The Gift of Light" quickly became one of David's favorites. He placed a large copy of it on the wall in front of his desk, and often uses this picture as a discussion point for sharing with curious visitors. This photograph presented after Alex asked the *Myst*, "What does God look like?"

In the upper right of the picture a large face is outlined with *Myst*. Out of the mouth area flows brighter white *Myst* (Fluff with Light Striations). This white *Myst* seems to generate a pattern that is presented in pink (more Cloud), and again, a face can be discerned in this pink bounded shape which, in turn, seems to blend into a white-moving-into-blue group of smaller patterns (Cloud) captured at the bottom left of the picture. Upon a closer look, a face can also be seen in the middle top of the bright white *Myst* form, and once that face is located it's easy to imagine outstretched arms of this *Myst* figure. Thus the "breath" coming out of the larger face appears to be formed and shaped into another figure with arms outstretched, and the focus of both the larger and smaller (brighter) figure is on the shapes to the left of the picture which are bounded in pink, and then move into a blue tint.

In the Myst-Art Gallery, this photograph is described as:
"And then it was said, 'Let there be light.' And there was."

Situated to the south, the direction of the photograph represents (among other attributes) purification, faith, strength, awakening of inner child and resurrection (Andrews, 2005).

* * * * *

David:

When I looked at this picture for the first time, my eyes immediately fell on the pink area which looked like a face looking upward at a small pattern directly in front of it. The face shows one eye, a high forehead, what looks like long hair flowing down the back of the head, a strong, straight nose, and a mustache and beard. It reminded me of someone, but I could not remember who. The face seemed to be looking at what appeared to be a person walking up a steep hill or incline. When I used a flashlight to clarify the pattern, I was astounded! The figure was that of a small man (or perhaps elf) with two legs clearly shown, his left arm bent at the elbow across his chest, his right arm hanging down, and the face reflecting a beard, two eyes (white spots) and a cap with a tassel. Behind the figure there appeared to be two other figures (people), but it was difficult to identify distinguishing features.

After the shock that the *Myst* had presented to us with such patterns and knowing that these patterns could not have been randomly produced because of the probability discussed in Chapter 2, I became fascinated by what we had experienced. Could this pattern of a small man have been randomly produced? From any point of view the answer seems to be "no."

Recall earlier we described information as any non-random pattern and certainly this pattern of a small man is information. The basic question is: What does the picture tell us? What does it mean? Can we learn anything from it? Is there some intelligence behind the *Myst* that created this pattern and perhaps is trying to communicate information, knowledge or even wisdom? Wouldn't it be wonderful if this were the case? How can we find out? How do we know? To date, from Alex's and my viewpoint, we simply don't know, but there is this repeated evidence which leads us to keep our minds open to pursue to the fullest what we are experiencing, and to continue to expand our understanding of both the science of the *Myst* and the nature of this aspect of spirituality.

Regarding the pink face in the picture just described, it appears to closely resemble Michelangelo's painting of God on the ceiling of the Sistine Chapel in Rome. Of course, this could be coincidence or wishful thinking. We know there are studies that indicate that what we see is strongly influenced by what we want to see. Our feelings, beliefs and goals may heavily influence our perceptions and thereby create our reality. On the other hand, by being aware of this, I had not previously seen Michelangelo's vision painted in 1508 of the creation of man. The two pictures are certainly not identical, but they do have many characteristics in common, enough to make me wonder. Is there a message in the patterns? Possibly. It is easy to create a plausible story: the pink face of God is observing mankind as humanity tries to climb up the steep hill of evolution and progress, thwarted by the challenges and rough spots of the material world and by its own fallibilities and internal shortcomings. Hard, if not impossible, questions to answer. Yet? Questions are often far more important than answers, since answers close off learning and questions lead to thinking, creativity and insights—that often lead to more questions, but with a deeper comprehension of the situation.

We are all aware of our modern challenge to create a safe inhabitable world for our children and hopefully most of the life forms currently on earth. Could this photograph of the *Myst* be a warning or just the imagination of an old physicist? There are other patterns in this picture that are take-off platforms for possibilities, preferabilities and probabilities. Of themselves, they do not prove anything (in terms of scientific proof), yet they invite further inquiry, deeper thinking, new perspectives, and a closer relationship with the spiritual part of the Universe as well as with our own souls. By soul I mean the animating and vital principle in each of us or, as Csikszentmihalyi says, "the energy a person or organization devotes to purposes beyond itself." (Csikszentmihalyi, 2003, p. 19)

Looking in the upper right corner of the picture, we can perceive a large dark face with two eyes looking down upon the scene below. The face appears to be breathing light down to the pink face. This dark face could represent our Universe. The light is the information created and stored within the Universe, with the pink face representing some concept that we think of as God with the little man representing the human species or perhaps all of Life. Does this one interpretation make much sense? Perhaps, or perhaps not. It depends on each of our own belief systems and the scope and depth of our knowledge in this field of experience and learning.

My point is that if these patterns are not random then they will contain some level of information and, if possible, we should try our absolute best to comprehend that information, recognizing that my interpretation may or may not be "right." More likely it is off base, but (and this is a capital "BUT"), the real value will come from our attempts to integrate, understand and make whatever sense we can of what we observe. If what we observe does NOT make sense, then *we* need to learn more about the situation observed and the methodology of observation. We must not write off the phenomenon as flawed and nonexistent because of our own incapacities, or because we simply do not know.

* * * * *

Scientists from theoretical physics to cosmotologists are still trying to figure out what really makes up our world and this Universe. In his 2010 book *The Grand Design*, world renown physicist Stephen Hawkins pointed out the challenges and difficulties of comprehending what he calls model-dependent realism. There is no one model that explains all of reality, and the more we learn about our world the more confusing and surprising it appears. Recognizing what we do not know or understand is critical to our willingness to learn, understand and keep an open mind. As David likes to say, there is no such thing as absolute knowledge.

CHILD OF THE UNIVERSE

Taken in front of the main house, an extraordinary *Myst* photograph is that of a baby wrapped in a blanket. (See next page.) Note that the child and blanket are both pink (Cloud with some Fluff) while the figure holding the child is white *Myst* (Circles). Upon close examination facial features of the baby can be identified. The larger figure presenting the child appears to be wearing a cowl, indicative of a monk's hooded cloak, with the face barely discernible under the hood. (See the discussion on Cloaked Visitors below.) There are also some pink highlights in the Fluff *Myst* swirling below the child in the lower left part of the picture. The symbolism of a child is new life, new beginnings. There is also a nurturing element conveyed by a cloaked figure holding the infant and the wrappings or swaddling clothes around the infant. The child and its wrappings are a different texture and color (pink) than the larger *Myst* figure holding the child. Can this be a coincidence?

The backdrop of the picture shows perpendicular, connecting fences, with red ribbons indicative of the Christmas timeframe. Because of the prominence of this background, the picture can be identified as appearing to the East of the photographer. East represents healing, creativity, illumination, divination, and new birth (Andrews, 2005). Is this a coincidence?

 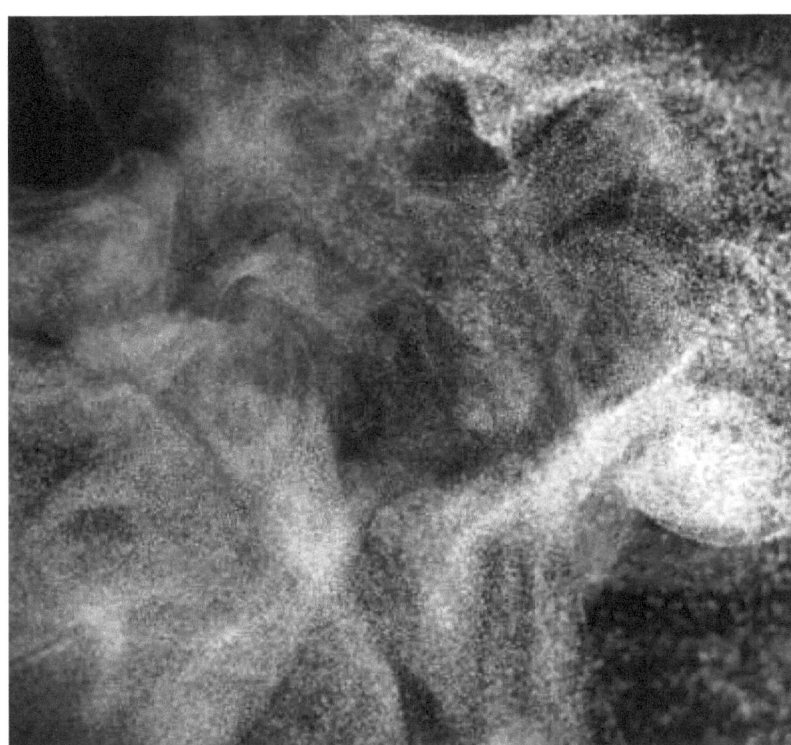

(Left) The description of this photograph is "The Myst honors the gift of life as the Universe expands." Note the monk's hooded cloak, which is the subject of our next conversation. (Right) Each swirl of the mane on this Myst picture of Zatara can be interpreted as a cloaked figure. Several faces are discernible.

CLOAKED VISITORS

The first time the Cloaked Visitors appeared in a picture was in the mane of beautiful Zatara, a picture introduced in Chapter 7. Looking closely at the photograph, there are numerous Cloaked Visitors whose hoods add to the swirl of the mane.

Once aware of these figures, Alex and David began to identify them in other pictures. For example, a Cloaked Visitor is a rider of the *Myst* in the photograph to the right, and is similar to the smaller cloaked figures that make up Zatara's mane. As described in "Child of the Universe" above, there is the perception of a cowl, indicating the possibility of a monk's hooded cloak. There is almost an echo to the left which insinuates the possibility of another rider behind the front one. Note there are marks for the eyes, a nose and mouth. While the *Myst* is primarily Cloud in texture, as often happens part of the *Myst* shapes (top of the *Myst* steed and on the rider's cloak) have a faint hint of Circle texturing. Upon close examination, there are multiple potential faces on the back of the *Myst* steed.

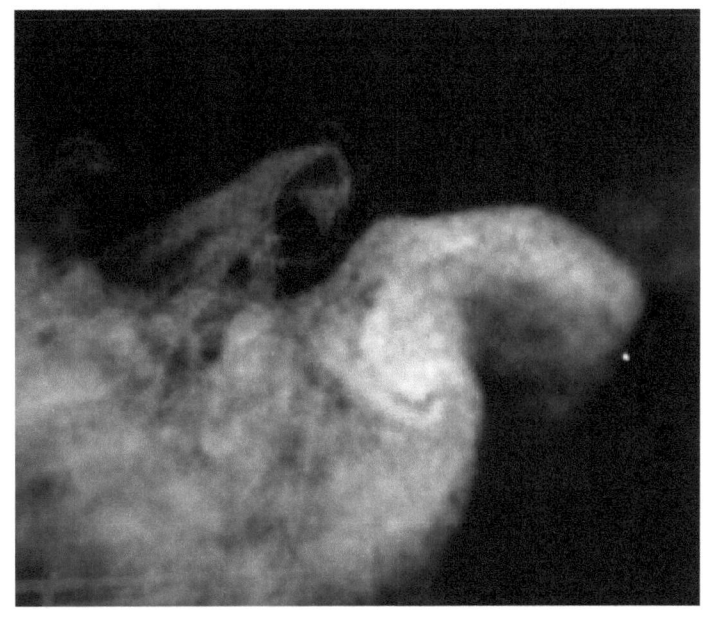

A Cloaked Visitor rides atop a Myst steed.

It wasn't until the Fall of 2011 that Alex began to see a resemblance in the Cloaked Visitors in the *Myst* photographs and David when he was working out with the animals wearing a hooded sweatshirt. While the Cloaked Visitors in Zatara's mane may be difficult to see in the small picture in this eBook, the picture below is larger. To the left is a hooded picture of David. To the right is a larger picture of a *Myst* Cloaked Visitor. When Alex looked at David with his hood on while he was feeding the farm animals, she recognized the close resemblance to the Cloaked Visitors in other photographs. If you look closely, you can see a resemblance in the face, that is, the accent of a mustache and a possible beard below the mouth. Of course, that's the way the mind works. We store patterns in invariant form, then fill in the rest during the moment at hand.

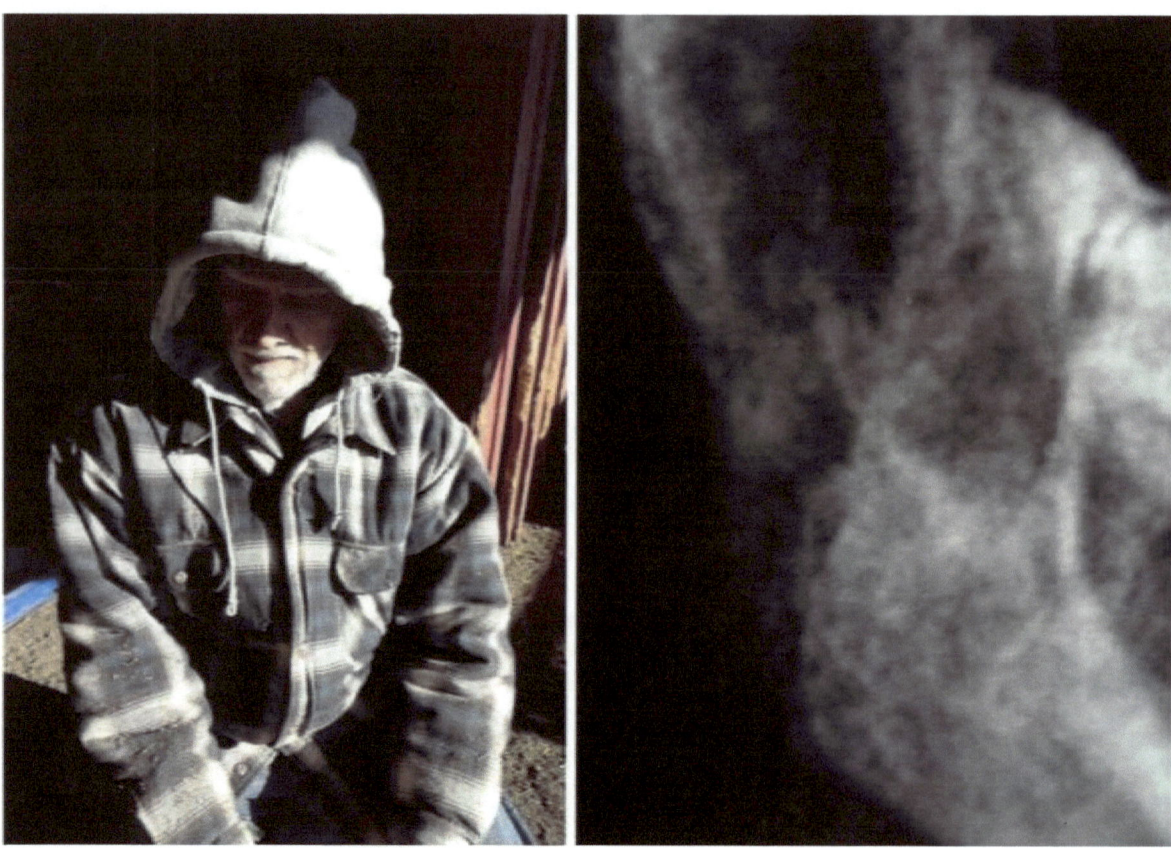

Alex felt that David in his hooded jacket in front of the barn showed some resemblance to the Cloaked Visitors appearing in her photographs.

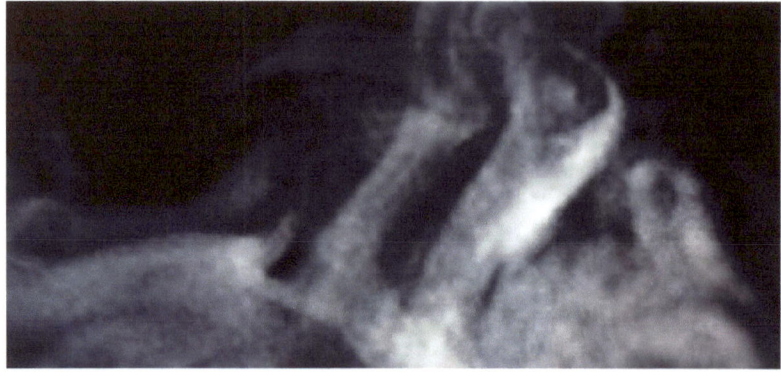

Do you remember the pattern of "tubes" introduced in the first chapter? Clearly, these cloaked figures bear a resemblance to the pattern of tubes. So, let's take a close look. Do there appear to be faces in the top of the "tubes" pattern? Perhaps. Unfortunately, our pixilation is not clear enough to clarify that since the picture will become fuzzier as you enlarge it. Still, the idea is worth contemplating.

MUSIC AND RHYTHM IN THE *MYST*

For Alex, who had a passion for opera singing in the early years of her life, it was exciting to discover the representation of music and rhythm in the *Myst*. This takes a variety of forms, sometimes conveyed through swirling *Myst* that appeared to be dancing and other times through more formal figures who take the shape of musicians.

* * * * *

Alex:

It became increasingly clear that it was impossible to take the viewer out of the translation—nor did we really want to! As we viewed each picture searching for meaning, we kept asking: What does this mean to me? While sometimes the answers to this question would result in agreement between David and I, most of the time we saw different things in the pictures, and different pictures grabbed our attention. We went with the flow, printing off copies of the pictures that we liked, looking at them daily, and jotting down feelings as they occurred.

These pictures became very personal, touching our lives in surprising ways which will be detailed in the third book in this series, *The Mind and the Myst*. Often, we saw that which was familiar, although not altogether expected! For example, in my early life I was a musician; I had a passion for opera and my first husband was a violinist and composer. What a delightful surprise when I recognized him in the *Myst* holding a violin! (That's his face in the upper left.) While the *Myst* primarily presents as Cloud there are noticeable Circles and Pocked effects. (Could there be several cloaked figures in the middle top or are those circles/eyes of a larger figure?) Near the center of the picture there are several Light Striations. Are they perhaps dancing to the music?

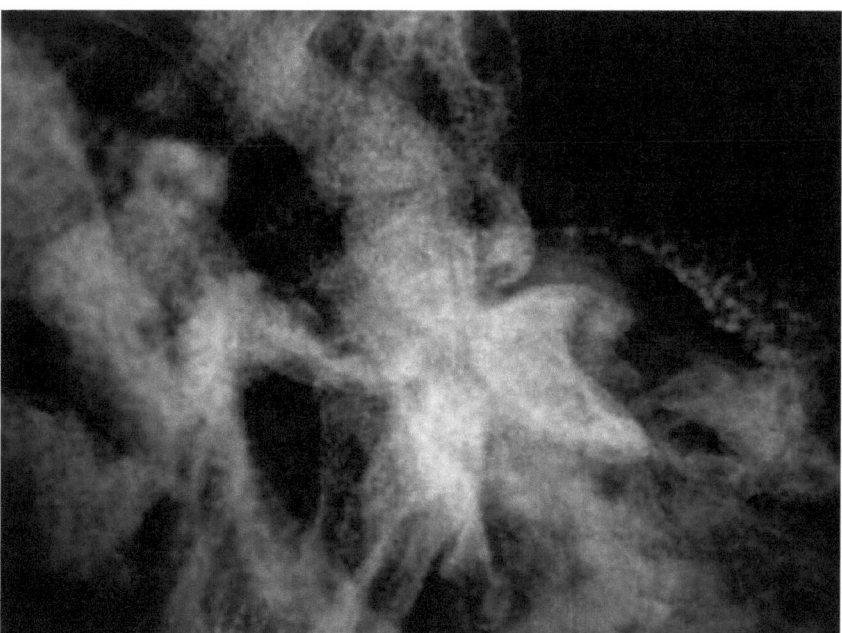

In the Myst-Art Gallery this photograph is titled "Meeting and Greeting" and is described: "In the garden midsummer night playing a tune as fairy Myst dances and twirls."

But it didn't stop there. I love the music of the harp and sure enough a harpist appeared in the *Myst*. I could almost hear the music, although undoubtedly it was my imagination.

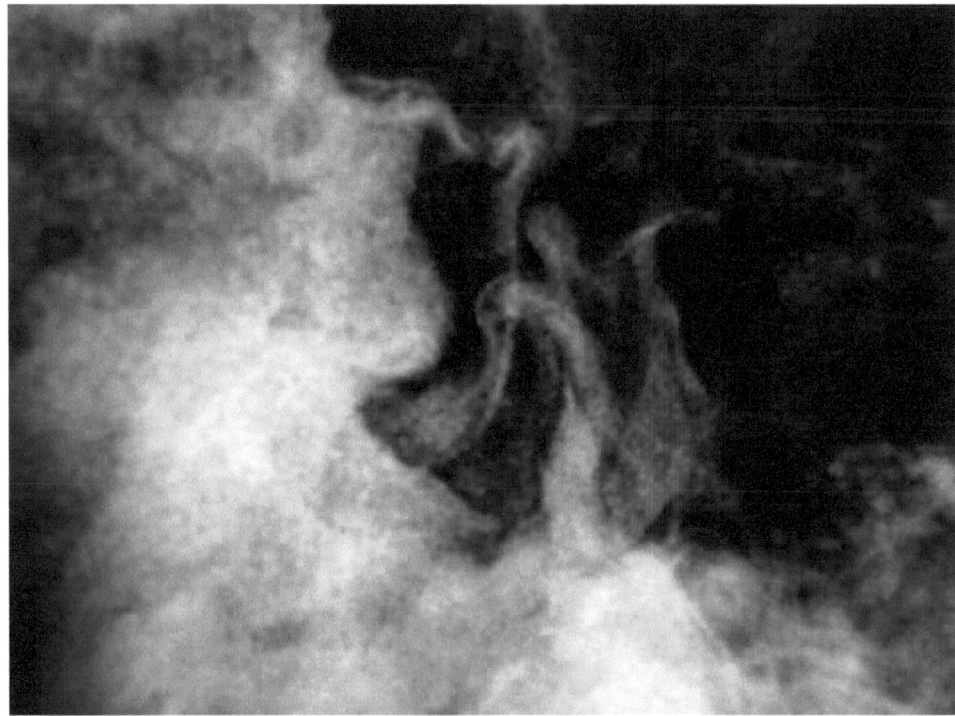

This photograph is part of the collection titled "Music of the Spheres" in the Myst-Art Gallery. The photographs are centered around the message: "The music of the spheres dances with light and love, sending resonances to the human mind and heart, and reminding us that we all vibrate in one Universe."

There were other musicians who joined the fun! And, of course, there had to be a piper, similar to the "Pied Piper" concept, sending mellow tones unheard by our ears out across the Universe. The *Myst* presents as Cloud.

 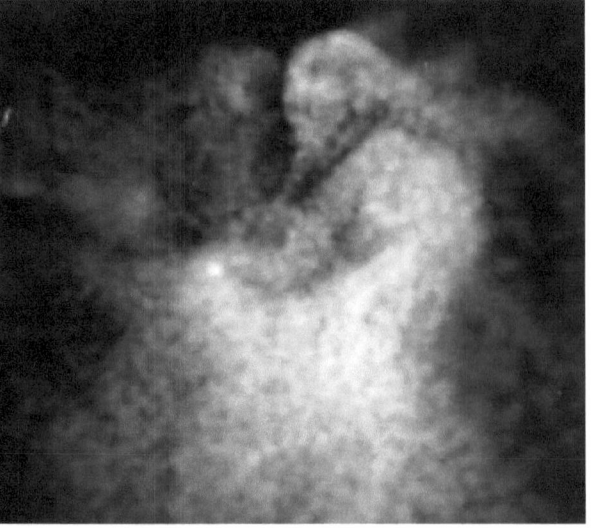

(Left) This photograph is also part of the collection titled "Music of the Spheres" in the Myst-Art Gallery. (Right) The Pied Piper in the Myst.

When I first began to touch the "Heavens" in my internal journey, I visualized myself in a wonderful cathedral listening to the music of the angels. Now, as my internal and external worlds continue to collide, how wonderful to have these *Myst* representatives bring their Heavenly music down to Earth.

* * * * *

CROWNED WITH LIGHT

The photograph we named "Crowned with Light" has layers and layers of shapes and patterns. For example, at the upper left of this photograph there appears to be a face wearing a crown (this was introduced in Chapter 5). At the lower right a number of faces appear, almost suggesting a "choir" or support group of some nature. The *Myst* in this picture presents primarily as Fluff, although there are elements of Cloud in the lower right and upper left, and displays a wonderful entanglement of pinks and whites. Let's take a few minutes to look more closely at this photograph, explore its patterns, and perhaps uncover some meaning.

This photograph titled "Crowned with Light" in the Myst-Art Gallery is described:
"The majesty of communing in the Myst: one voice, one song, one heart."

Recall the sphere has been recognized throughout history as reflecting power (see Chapter 1 Introduction). The crown is a political manifestation that represents a sphere around the head, a sign of responsibility and equanimity, "showing the subtle transfer of meaning between geometry and the evolution of consciousness" (Volk, 1995, p. 22). For example, in 1610 one theoretician wrote of James I of England:

> *The Sphear-like forme of his Crowne doth denote the even roundnesse wherein he proceedeth to every one, as well towards, the small as the great, the poore as well as the rich ... like unto the Geometrical point, which beholdeth all his circumference in one and the same proportion.* (Craig, 1951)

Here's what a long-time colleague in the Knowledge Management field and frequent visitor to Mountain Quest has to say about this photograph.

* * * * *

Susan:

"Crowned with Light" is one of the most spiritual and evocative photographs I have ever seen. I have a copy of it, and keep it out where others can see it. It has brought people to tears, made their hearts fly with excitement they could barely express, and caused them to stand in front of it for a good length of time in what could only be described as prayer. When Alex shared this photo with me, I could see many, many faces of several races and many ages in it as well as animals of all kinds. Over time the images seem to be changing, some going away, others emerging. It is both very strange and extremely exciting. When I meditate on this photo, I feel sort of "crowned with light" myself, close to Source, joined with life energy, and that Alex and David have discovered a truth, a knowledge that we are not alone. Our brains filter out so much visual information that is right there in front of us, perhaps out of necessity, perhaps we are not ready to make sense of all of it. I have spent time digging for meaning, and will spend much more time doing so.

* * * * *

There are SO MANY interesting and intriguing *Myst* photographs to explore and share. But ultimately, it is you who must decide how you "feel" about the *Myst*, what you "think" a particular picture represents, the meaning behind that picture, and what this phenomenon says about the Universe and our place in it. But before we move into the physics of the *Myst*, let's look at some of the pictures that Alex and David interpret as angels.

Chapter 8: A Stream of Angels

For those who embrace their spiritual nature, the appearance of angels is the quintessence of dreams come true. The word angel, derived from the Greek word *angelos*, translates as "messenger of God." Because of the Renaissance paintings reproduced in books, religious art and on special occasion cards, we have expectations of seeing angels in flowing garments with wings and halos, and indeed many of the *Myst* angels portray this historical archetype.

As Alex sang to bring in the *Myst*, her expression of joy often rang out as, "Beautiful angels in the *Myst*, come into my picture please tonight" or a variation on these words. Little wonder that when wings began to show up on *Myst* figures these were quickly described as angels. Through the months there has been a continuous stream of angels, some clearly captured and others fanned by Alex's interpretation. In the process of opening her mind and tuning her senses to this previously unseen world of energy, Alex was able to bring visible angels into her everyday life.

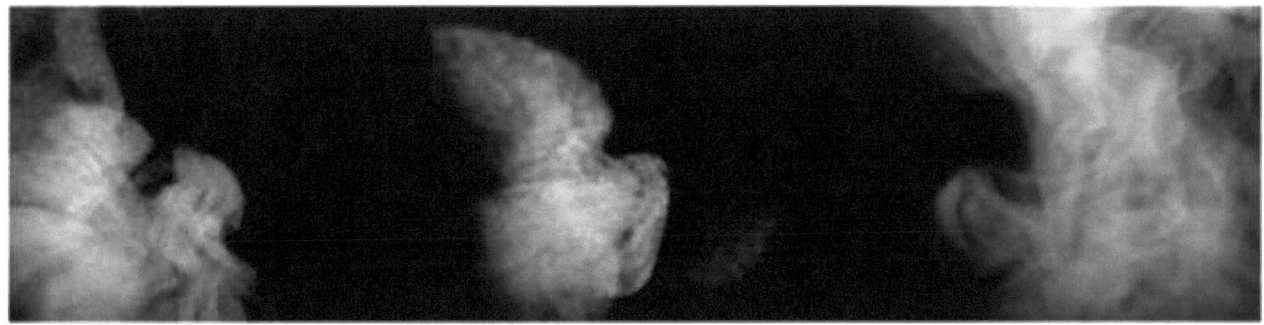

A stream of angelic Myst forms, each appearing on a separate occasion.
Several of these will be discussed below.

Along this incredible journey into the *Myst*, Alex began to look for wing spans, and it is those angelic figures with wings that are the subject of this chapter. For example, the right wing of the middle angel in the photograph stream above is stretched out toward the top of the picture. This wing is clearly Circles, although the lower part of the picture presents as Cloud. Upon investigation, there appears to be a smaller face and a larger face in the middle of the shape.

The angel to the right provides the feeling of a figure in flight with wings widespread. Although the texture of this *Myst* figure is Fluff, it presents with a soft semi-gloss look (soft light). This photograph was used as a Christmas offering with the words "We bring you glad tidings" embedded in the *Myst* wing.

While Alex daily called on angels to come into her pictures, the largest number of photographs she has taken are of Guide Clouds. Of course, in Alex's mind and heart her guides ARE angels, although they do not display wings and seem to be joined by a shared core cloud of *Myst*.

The photograph below is a compilation also prepared as a Christmas offering with Cloud Guides along the lower part of the picture and several angelic forms above. The angel to the upper left appears in flight with flowing garments. Is there something specific carried in the hands? It's hard to tell. The *Myst* is primarily Cloud in nature with hints of Fluff.

And all the Angels in Heaven and Earth Sang and Rejoiced ...

This compilation of Myst figures was prepared as a Christmas offering in the Myst-Art gallery. The lower grouping appears to be holding a banner, although the message (if any) is indiscernible.

The wingspan is also expressed from a sideward direction. In the photograph below, this sideward view of an angel with wings extending to the back also presents as a "dove" in the front part of the angel. Note that the face has two marks where eyes would appear in the shaped head, and in the lower dove figure there are also visible eyes. While the texture of this *Myst* angel and the dove is Cloud, upon closer inspection Circles can be recognized in the less opaque parts of the *Myst*.

In Alex's belief set, each human has one or more guardian angels that stay with us for our entire lives. These angels nudge us to make choices consistent with our highest Self and comfort us when we're sad, frustrated, disappointed, feeling helpless or lonely.

(Right) In the Myst-Art Gallery this photograph is described as: "Wings of Myst shadow this angelic form, sending love."

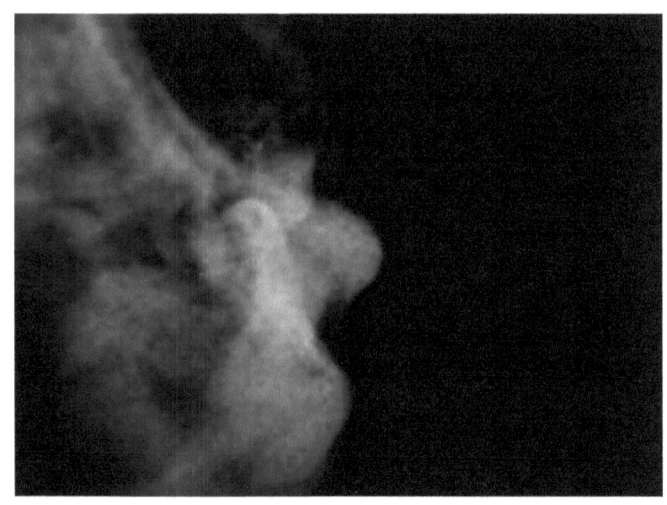

The delightful full winged angel shown below is titled "Guardian Angel" in the *Myst*-Art Gallery. While the head is darker, two eyes are distinct. The right wing is extended to the tip, the left wing appears to extend backwards. The figure is primarily Cloud with the representation of Circles throughout the left wing and upper tip of the right wing. This picture is part of the angel stream presented in the beginning of this chapter.

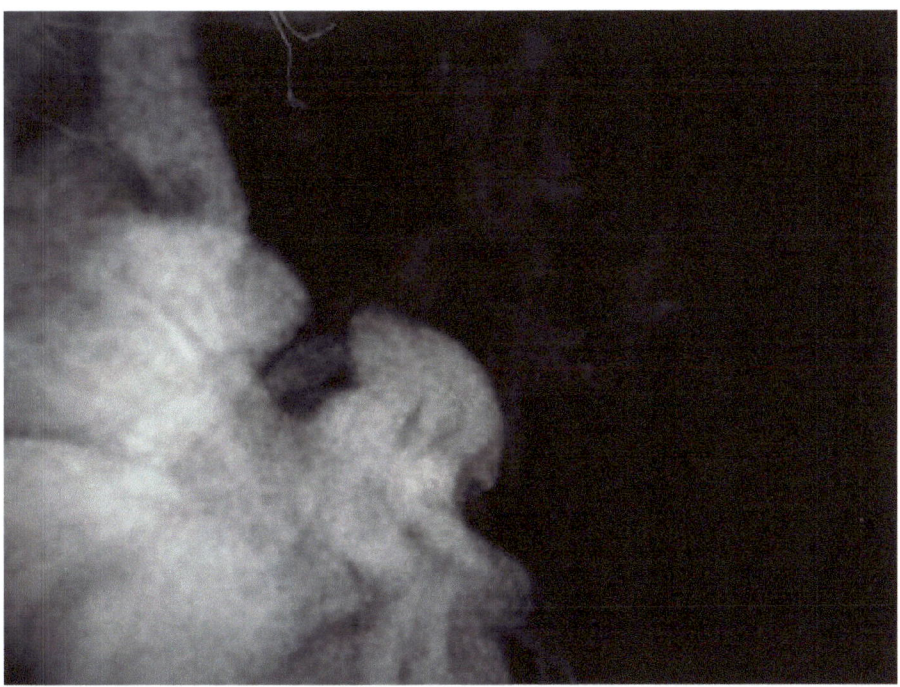

In the Myst-Art Gallery this photograph is described:
"With unfurled wings an angelic form hovers above, ready to intercede."

Angels do not always appear alone, but rather as part of a scene that is conveying a message. For example, in the photograph below, a kneeling angel is delivering a message to another *Myst* figure. The *Myst* is Circles with a splash of Bright Light. In addition to the face of the messenger, several faces are visible in the right middle of the photograph, including a darker face with two eye marks, a mouth and dark hair. When this photograph was captured it gave off a blue glow, which might well be due to the particular angle of the camera during a full-moonlit night.

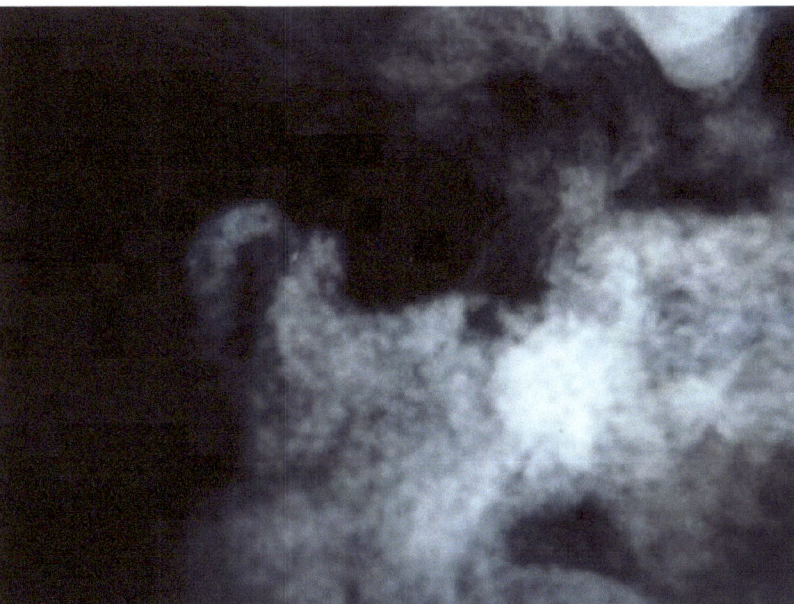

(Left) This photograph is titled "The Messenger" in the Myst-Art gallery and is described as "An angelic messenger, perhaps delivering news of a pending birth."

MYST ANGELS WRAPPED IN PINKS

In a stream such as this one it is difficult to figure out groupings. One interesting aspect of the *Myst* is the periodic presence of pinks as accents or part of the *Myst* angel itself. In the previous chapter, the "Child of the Universe" appeared in pink. An example of an angelic scene with pink accents is "Angel at Large" (shown in the photograph below). The *Myst* is primarily Fluff with Light Striations. This picture can be viewed in many different ways. A guest who attends the Mormon church sees this picture as a rendition of the Angel Moroni, who was the guardian of the golden plates. The Angel Moroni is usually pictured with hand extended blowing a long horn.

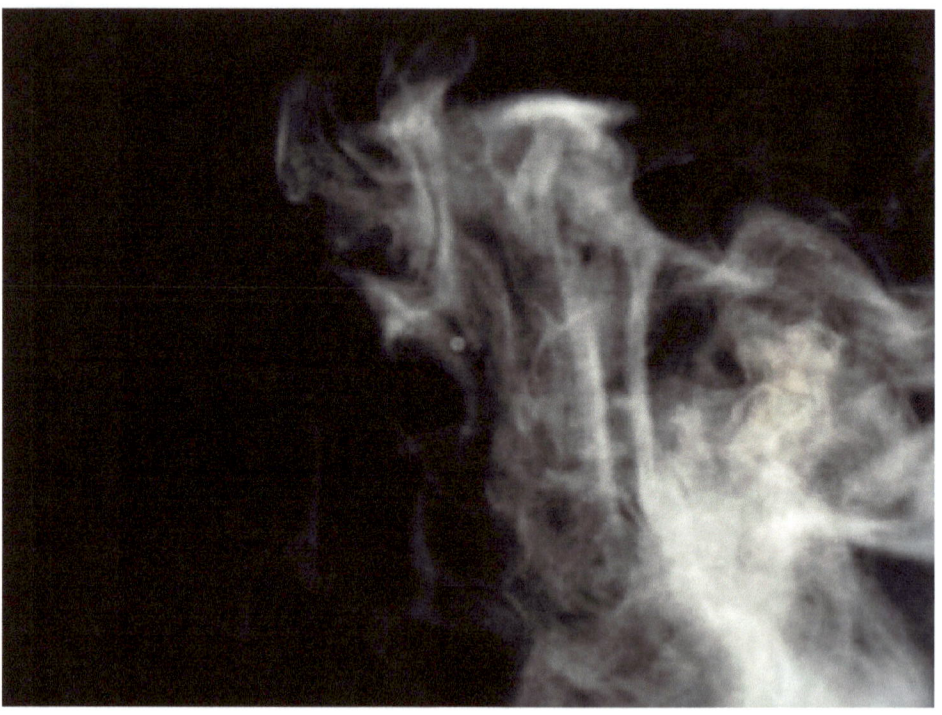

(Above) This photograph is titled "Angel at Large" in the Myst-Art Gallery and is described as: "Always close at hand waiting for your call for assistance."

From another perspective, the angel can be perceived as located in the middle of the picture, with the face in the upper middle and an oval halo above the head. This style halo was painted by many Renaissance artists. For example, this same treatment of the halo appears in Andrea del Verrocchoi's rendition of "Tobias and the Angel", an altar painting finished around 1470-1480 housed in the National Gallery of London.

(Right) A cropped portion of "Tobias and the Angel" painted by Andrea del Verrocchio as an altar painting and now housed in the National Gallery of London. Leonardo da Vinci was a member of Verrocchio's studio and may have painted some part of this work. Note the similarity of the oval halo in the "Angel at Large" Myst photograph.

The Archangel Michael is in the order of angels called "Virtues" and is a leader among archangels. Michael exudes a warrior-like presence. He is a protector for all those who call upon him as well as the overseer and inspirer of the lightworkers here on Earth (Virtue, 2003). When he first appeared to Alex on October 6, 2010, he was a deep pink in color—almost purple—and stood about 15 feet high. In the darkness his body and wings appeared to be somewhat translucent and the strong face with distinct features seemed to be mirrored at the back of the head. His *Myst* body was primarily Fluff, but with a crystalline look. This is the angel who caused Alex to ask "Should I be afraid?" and whose touch in response filled Alex with waves of love (see *The Journey into the Myst*). Alex was intrigued with the pink representation since archangel Michael is generally portrayed with blue.

(Above) The first angel to appear to Alex was perceived as Archangel Michael. However, later she had the "feeling" that it was Archangel Raphael. He was about 15 feet high and fierce looking.

Later that fall another angel appeared with pink accents throughout the *Myst* figure, punctuated by alternating soft light and bright light presenting in Fluff. This angel appears to convey a seriousness in the primary face, although there are softer faces visible throughout the wings. Note that Alex felt love and joy during ALL of her *Myst* experiences.

(Right) This photograph is titled "Overlooking" in the Myst-Art Gallery with the description: "An Angelic force with unfurled wings calls for a command performance."

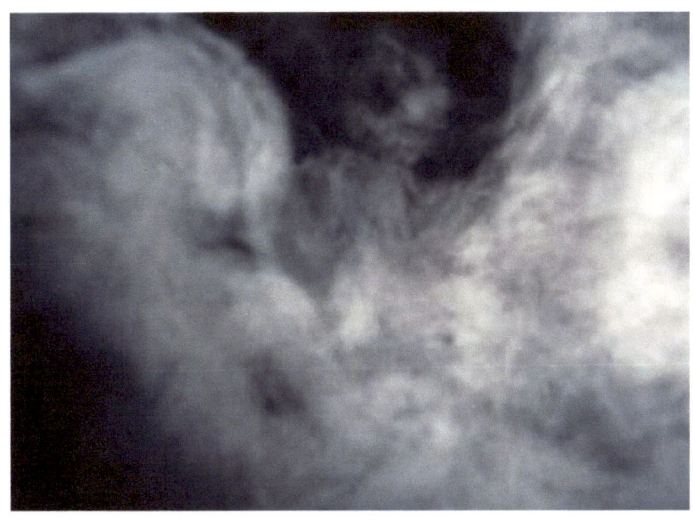

Perhaps one of the most amazing photographs of a *Myst* angel, accented in pinks, is that which Alex attributes as Mother Theresa (see *The Journey into the Myst*). The light of the angel herself was so bright that the camera was unable to pick up all of the characteristics in the Bright Light pattern. However, the overall shape jumps out of the picture, and the long hair coming down around the face and neck is discernible. There is also a hint of facial features. Around the main figure there were bursts of pink light textured as Fluff and Cloud, several with the translucent quality of Soft Light.

 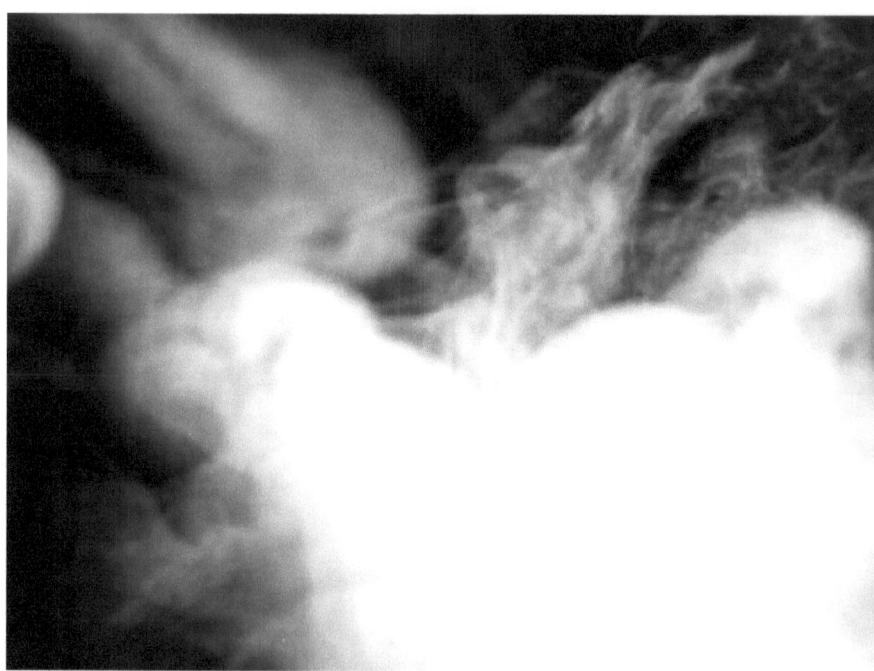

(Right) This picture was titled "Mother of Mercy, Angel of Light" in the Myst-Art Gallery. It is the featured photo on a special offering combined with 1984 pictures of Mother Teresa taken by Alex in Japan. One of these photographs is above to the left.

Alex describes the light as similar to that of a full moon on a very clear night. Her eyes were drawn to that bright light such that there was not enough time to capture the essence of the wonderful moving pink light around the main figure.

So, the question remains: What is the significance of pink (colors ranging from a bluish red or purple to red) in the *Myst*? Let's explore various possibilities. First, pink is generally recognized as the color of love. In Catholicism pink (called rose by the Catholic Church) symbolizes joy and happiness. Similarly, the rose quartz gemstone is known as the love stone and is an accelerator of compassion and universal love and, in general, pink gemstones are used to stimulate love and beauty.

Chapter 9: The Physics of the *Myst*

While we have drawn on the work of several physicists and other researchers in earlier chapters, a large part of what we have written is based on observation and the journals kept throughout those periods of observation. In this way we hope to better comprehend the meaning, nature and importance of the *Myst*. In other words, we are trying to increase our knowledge of what is happening.

We repeat a bit here to aid understanding of our thinking. In our professional work we defined knowledge as the capacity to take effective action; having the insight, intuition, judgment and foresight to understand, interact with and influence a system or situation in a way that will result in the best outcome. We take understanding as perceiving and/or comprehending the nature and significance of some event or phenomenon. Comprehension is the act of grasping the meaning, nature or importance of some event or phenomenon. Relative to the *Myst*, we are just beginning to have some knowledge—but the challenge and potential result may be well worth the effort. Actually, it is already well worth the effort ... but that is our third book.

While the scientific part of the *Myst* may still need much research, the spiritual part may offer far greater rewards and opportunities if we can only begin to recognize the meaning and potential of what is happening. The Universe is so big, and we are so small; it seems foolish and possibly dangerous to ignore (or discount) possibilities because they are not consistent with what we call our "material world."

It should be noted that our "material world" is not made up of solid objects, but of energy and patterns of energy caused by the four fundamental forces: electromagnetic, gravity, nuclear and weak nuclear. These four forces are found widely throughout the cosmos and are consistent with our understanding of the molecular physical reality (as differentiated from Tiller's second physical reality based on magnetic resonance). The electromagnetic field (what we normally think of as light) is omnipresent throughout the Universe in varying levels of intensity; we as humans are able to see only a very small fraction of the full spectrum of frequencies that make up light. With electromagnetic energy, the nuclear forces between nucleons in atoms (neutrons, protons), the weak nuclear force (operating within the nucleus of atoms) and gravity make up the four fundamental forces which science has identified in the molecular physical reality of the Universe. Note that while in pragmatic terms we think of gravity as a force attracting masses, the current interpretation of gravity is a warping of space.

As a human species we have much to learn—that is, we must be cautious about thinking we have absolute knowledge or believing we are sure we are right and that others are wrong in disagreeing with our interpretation of reality. With that in mind, we forward the following key learnings from our interactions with the *Myst*.

1. Water molecules are used to form the *Myst*.

Given that the *Myst* is formed from the electromagnetic energy of orbs assimilating and using water molecules, what exactly does this mean? How can this aid our understanding of the physical phenomenon of the *Myst*? The Chambers Dictionary of Science and Technology (1999) defines mist as "a suspension of water droplets (radii less than 1 μm or one millionth of a meter) reducing the visibility to not less than 1 km (or one thousand meters. We spell "mist" as "myst" because of the beauty and mystery behind the pictures; we shall continue to do so.

Water molecules have two hydrogen atoms and one oxygen atom held together by the attractive forces between these three atoms. These forces are somewhat complex, a combination of electron repulsion and van der Wall's attraction forces (Fraser, 2006). They are not symmetric, but consist of one oxygen atom with the two hydrogen atoms each about 1 Å from the oxygen atom but separated from each other at an angle of 104°. 1 Å (Amgstrom) is a very small distance! This non symmetric shape is very important because it allows the molecule to form clusters. As Pruppacher and Klett (1997) have noted, water molecules in water vapor form tend to interact and form clusters, which is in contrast to ideal gas behavior.

> *Recent experiments involving molecular beam techniques ... suggest that in highly supersaturated water vapor clusters up to 180 water molecules may be present. Clusters of 21 water molecules seem to exhibit particularly large stability. It is interesting to note that 21 water molecules can be arranged in a form of a pentagonal dodecahedron with a molecule at each corner and a single molecule in the center of the case.* (Pruppacher and Klett, 1997, p. 77)

This finding indicates that the molecules in the *Myst* have the capacity to create small clusters. These small clusters may create large and visually observable patterns of the *Myst* through the assimilation of clusters of water molecules, just as many different houses can be built from bricks where each brick could be considered a large group of small clusters of clay.

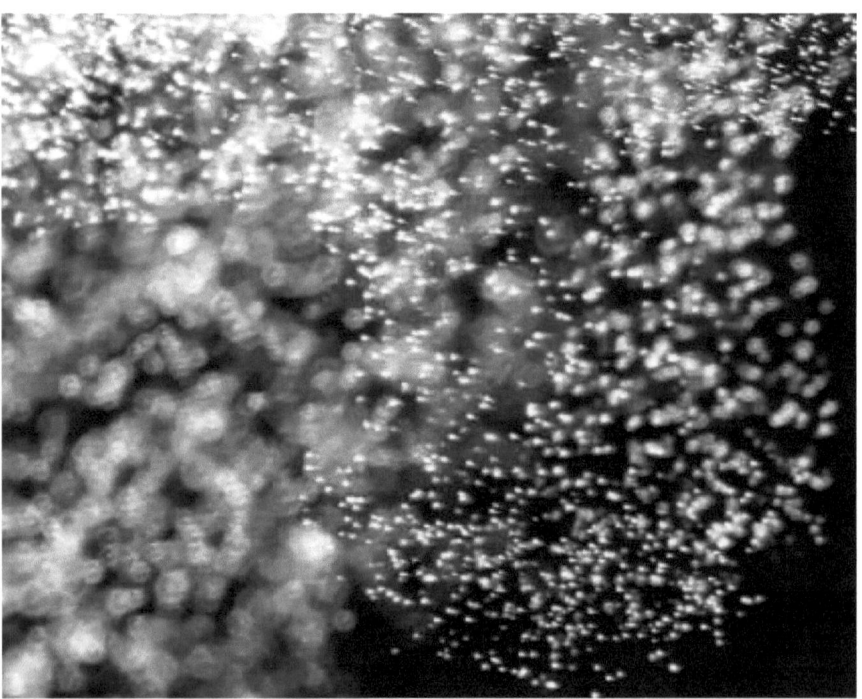

Orbs appear to expand through the assimilation of clusters of water molecules, then move together to form larger patterns of Myst which are visually observable. At the left this photograph shows the expanded orbs starting to cluster to form a larger shape.

From a material perspective, Rustum Roy, a well-published internationally known materialist scientist who works in one of the world's leading materials research laboratories, says that water is no longer considered "just water." At a recent U.S. National Academy of Engineering presentation titled "The Latest Science on Water," Roy pointed out that research scientists have concluded that there are 64 changes of water from one form to another, with nearly the same number of different structures. "There are certainly many, many different 'waters' with different structure and, therefore, different properties." (Roy, 2005)

Water is the single most important material for life on this planet, and probably on many other planets as well. Specifically, Rustin's presentation points out that water (H_2O) has no competitors and is the most anomalous, odd, peculiar, material on earth! For further reading on the amazing properties of water consider the references inserted throughout this chapter.

While the above does not prove the existence of *Myst* patterns in terms of meaning, it does lend credibility to the existence of water vapor (*Myst*) being able to take shapes and patterns as demonstrated in the large number of photographs taken by Alex at the Mountain Quest Institute. The huge unanswered question is, of course: What is the source (if any) that shapes and forms the patterns seen in the pictures?

2. Orbs are integral to forming the Myst

This follows from the section above. As introduced, the physics of water molecules allows the molecules (and hence the vapor) to connect together into structures which may then form larger patterns. Since water molecules (and hence mist) have electrons and protons within their shells and nuclei, they can be influenced by electromagnetic fields. Of the four known forces in the molecular Universe (introduced above), only the electromagnetic force would be sufficient to act on water molecules in the manner we are considering here.

Essentially, when the camera flash (photons) hit an Orb, the photons are absorbed by some of the molecules in the Orb; that is, electrons within the Orb absorb the photons which move them to a higher energy level within the Orb. When this occurs these electrons (in higher energy levels) fall back down to their current shell level and as they do so they radiate photons outward, and some of them to be absorbed by the camera. The colors (or energy) of the radiating electrons depend on the energy levels that the electrons are falling between. Since there are many levels available, many colors are created; this is what creates the beautiful, colorful orbs.

We view orbs as the primary source of electromagnetic energy that is influencing creation of the *Myst*. While orbs are not specifically the focus of this book, the *Myst* cannot be understood isolated from the Orb phenomenon. A number of researchers agree with our analysis that orbs are primarily comprised of electromagnetic energy. Of particular note is the thorough treatment of orbs by Míċeál Ledwith, a theologian who was professor of systematic theology and then president of Maynooth College in Ireland, and who served as a member of the International Theological Commission for seventeen years. See *The Orb Project* (Ledwith and Heinemann, 2007).

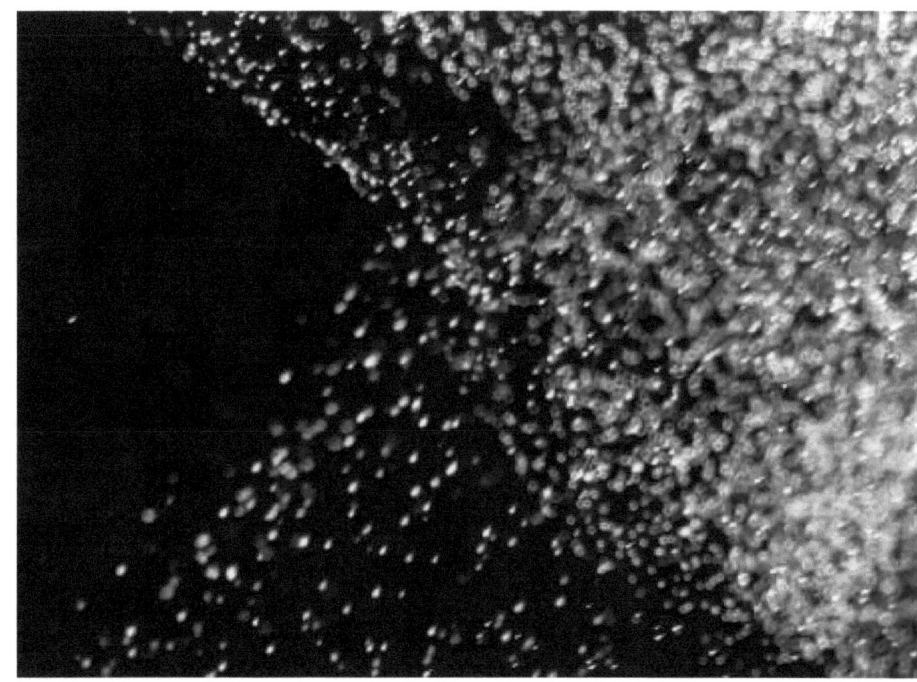

(Right) Orbs expanding into the Myst. See the Preface of this book for additional pictures of this phenomenon.

When studying the hexagonal forms that the orbs sometimes assumed, Ledwith discovered that their images were not due to reflected light from the camera flash, but from the generation of light within the orbs themselves. He felt this most likely occurred from the process of fluorescence which was triggered by the photons from the camera flash (as described above) and aided by an abundance of free electrons in the atmosphere from rainfall or the use of an ionizing apparatus or strobe. Ledwith's observations mean that the orbs which appear in these conditions must be electromagnetic in nature, and must also contain water vapor. Note that Alex has also captured orbs as hexagonal forms, and that the primary camera used to capture these Orb pictures has an infrared sensor light.

Approximately 70 percent of the *Myst* pictures Alex has taken have at least a part of the *Myst* shapes presented in Circles, which is strongly suggestive of their Orb makeup. Some of these photographs—happening in a millisecond (1000th of a second)—appear to capture the movement from orbs to Circles to Cloud textures, and sometimes all three exist in the *Myst* at the same time. In Chapter 3 we proposed a possible sequence, describing textures of the *Myst* as indicating levels of energetic involvement of the orbs. This sequence starts with orbs that (1) expand and come together to form and shape a larger essence (presenting as Circles). Then, as energy builds, (2) the circles become less prominent and present as Cloud forms. Then, as the energy continues to build (3) the Myst takes on the characteristics of Fluff, lighter, dancing with graceful curves and twists. As the energy builds even higher, (4) the Myst bursts into a firework of Dots, holding shape and form but conveying the beauty and magnificence of birth and potential. Finally (5) there is the possibility that Squirms are the visual representation of the *Myst* unforming.

This sequence—and the photographs demonstrating this sequence—demonstrate the direct relationship of orbs to the *Myst*. In other words, the orbs and the *Myst* are not only interrelated, but appear to be two aspects of an integrated phenomenon.

3. The *Myst* is affected by weather conditions.

Orbs appear to be around pretty much all the time. While Alex has not attempted to capture orbs during storms with heavy downpours, she has captured them inside and outside during times of rain, snow and fog. During light rain and snow, the orbs take on a Roy-G-Biv configuration, that is, they are bright white in the center with the colors of the spectrum moving from the edge on one side (low frequency, red color) and continuing at the edge on the other side (higher frequency, violet). The bright white in the center is an indicator of a higher level of energy (the sum of all colors), with the colors around the rims indicating less energy being radiated back to the camera.

(Above) Examples of orbs shooting through the snow.

As demonstrated by orbs caught in movement and presenting with "tails," the blue edge indicates the direction they are heading, and the red edge is the direction from which they come.

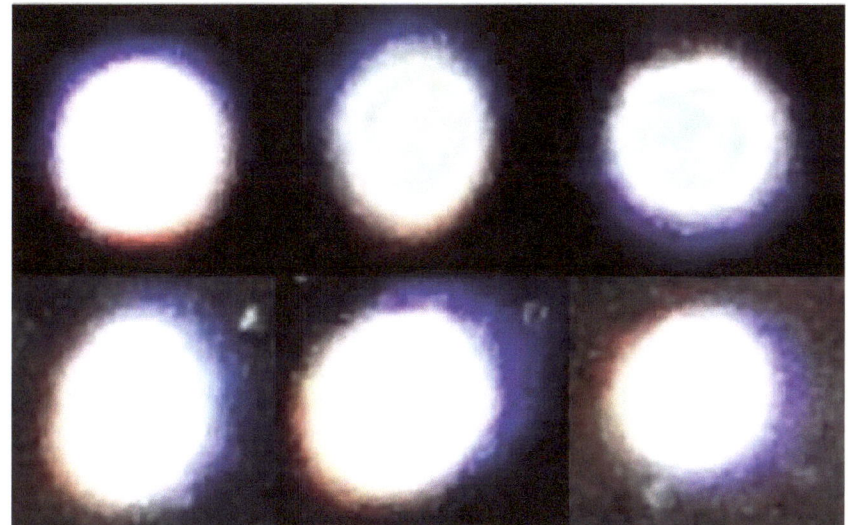

Alex thinks of the Roy-G-Biv configuration as a "mode," that is, a condition that all orbs assume when they are in a high-energy environment such as snow, regardless of the colors produced by the energy they generally radiate when photographed. Orbs shooting through the falling snow are included below.

Many of the photographers who capture Orb pictures would agree that there are more orbs present during rain and conditions of high humidity.

(Left) Several close-up photographs of orbs in the Roy-G-Biv mode.

Similarly, from observation over time, it appears that the non-randomness of the appearance of the *Myst* is affected by weather conditions. As recorded in Alex's journaling, it is clear that lower temperatures and higher levels of water in the air support continuous interaction with the *Myst*. This supported the thesis that the water in the air is an energy source used to form and shape the *Myst*. During rain and snow conditions, some pictures reflect holes where water or snowflakes have passed through the *Myst* (similar to pictures of orbs in these conditions). The appearance of *Myst* in the fog—and the disappearance of fog for the time period the *Myst* appeared—helped confirm the notion that the *Myst* was formed of water molecules in a mist state. See Alex's comments in Chapter 3 on this occurrence. Note that Alex gets excellent photographs of orbs "playing" in the fog.

This raises an interesting question about the phenomenon of breath on a cold day. Both Alex and David have purposefully taken pictures of their breath to compare with pictures of the *Myst*. While not always the case, on several occasions Alex's breath appeared to form shapes that had some of the same characteristics as the *Myst*. There is, of course, moisture in the breath, which would undoubtedly serve for the orbs the same purposes as mist. Another interesting point is a journal entry that occurred on several occasions where Alex commented that she could see a continuous sea of faces all around her in the darkness of the night. Alex began to believe that the faces were always there, yet the energies displayed through orbs and *Myst* certainly highlighted specific shapes and forms and faces.

In the closing of *Orbs Around the World: An Anthology*, editor Sandra Underwood expressed the questioning and doubt that most photographers of orbs and light waves (Sandra Underwood's term for the *Myst*) experience, specifically the response, "Oh, that is just your breath." Sandra eloquently responds:

> ... as if the very breath that is the sacred marker of being alive is to be discounted when the Light Beings respond to it and use it to co-create with us ... the images of light waves we see and feel and heal and learn from. (Underwood, 2011, p. 62)

While orbs can be photographed during a breeze (and Alex has repeatedly done so), the *Myst* does not appear during any significant level of wind conditions, but will rapidly appear when there is a moment of stillness from the wind. It is assumed that the lightness of the *Myst* would account for this. A difference in air pressure also appears to impact the *Myst*, with lower air pressure supporting clarity of the forms and shapes, that is, clarity of internal characteristics and external boundaries around *Myst* figures.

4. The *Myst* presents with a variety of energetic properties

The *Myst* appears in a great variety in size, boundaries, textures and color which suggest a great variety in energy relationships and densities.

SIZE AND BOUNDARIES. When Alex first began her interaction with the *Myst*, it appeared all around her for as far as she could see. There were large, flowing shapes which required a cramped neck to see the tops! It was only a few days of this before Alex said to the *Myst*, "If this is for me, you've got me! I believe! But if you want me to capture these pictures and share them, I need some clear boundaries. All I'm getting now is pictures full of light with various light striations across them." From that time onward the *Myst* presented (for the most part) about 2-3 feet in front of Alex with the size of the forms ranging from inches to several feet.

Note that size alone does not convey the meaning of the *Myst*. There have been several small circles of bright light that appeared directly before her lens that Alex described as "bright as the full moon, right here in front of my camera." These pictures conveyed specific scenes, often in answer to a specific question Alex had asked. For example, one of these was provided in response to Alex's request for her guides and angels to watch over Kumo, their 12-year-old Akita dog who had recently passed. This picture, shown below, is followed by a highlighted copy to facilitate meaning-making.

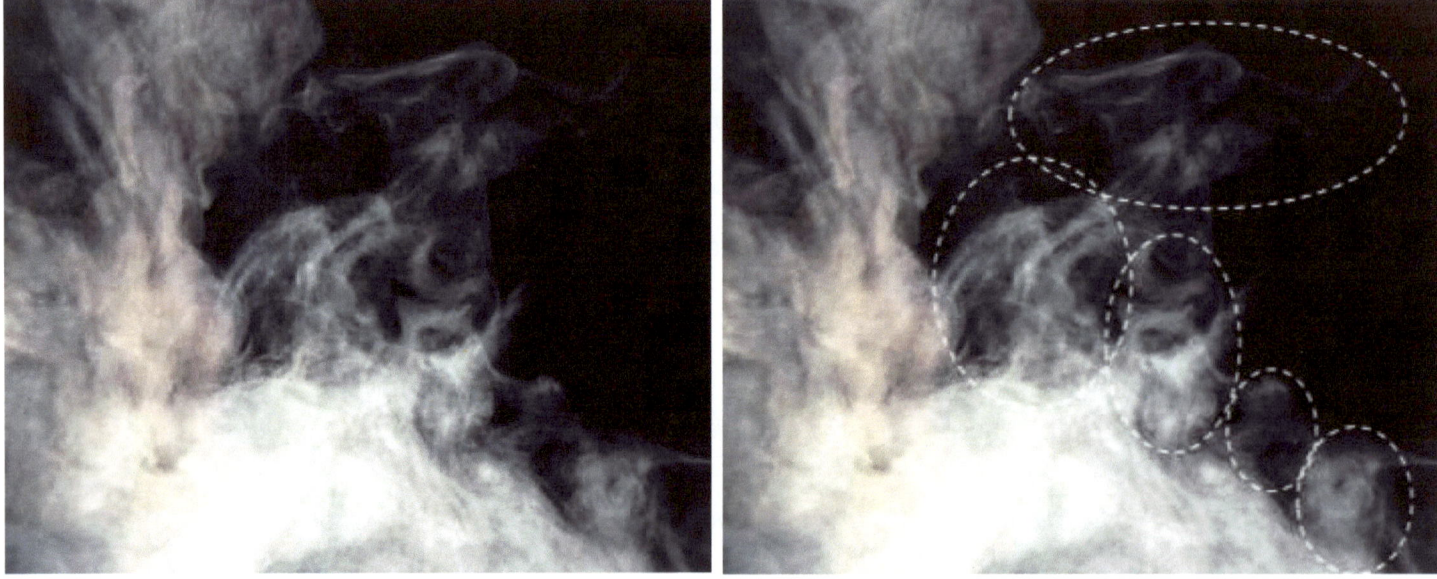

(Left) This photograph is entitled "The Journey Home." (Highlighted picture at right.) To the right at the bottom, you will note the profile of the top part of a human with hands clasped in prayer. Immediately in front of this figure to the left of the human shape is the large form of a dog. (Kumo weighed in at about 120 pounds.) Reaching to the neck where a dog collar would be located is a small angel bending toward the dog, appearing to be pulling him upward. Behind this small angel is the cloaked and bent figure of Mother Mary; standing right above Mother Mary is an angel with an open wing span. To the left is a swirl of pink energies that represent the Archangel of Compassion.

The boundaries of the *Myst* convey form and shape, sometimes with a clarity of stillness and other times suggesting movement. Some boundaries are very clean and others fuzzy. For an example of this contrast compare the picture provided in Chapter 3 for "Bounded and Rounded" and the picture above.

TEXTURES AND INTENSITY. The brightness or intensity of light conveyed in different *Myst* forms varies greatly. Different intensities would imply a higher density of water vapor and/or a closer distance between the *Myst* and the camera. The size of the pattern could also influence the perception of its intensity. As described in Chapter 3, the characteristics of Soft Light and Bright Light have specifically been identified in concert with various textures. Bright Light can appear as light striations across various textures. The various textures of the *Myst* appear to hold a clue to energy levels, with **the textures indicating the energetic involvement of the orbs**.

COLOR. The range of light in the electromagnetic spectrum is incredibly vast. When measured in octaves (with each octave doubling the frequency of the preceding one), there are over 60 octaves between the lowest and highest frequency waves. The visible light energy covers one octave on this scale. Isaac Newton's famous experiment with **refraction** showed all the colors of visible light—moving from a deep red through orange, yellow, green, blue, indigo and violet. These colors are directly related to wavelength and frequency. For example, visible light has a wavelength of 390 to 700 μm and a frequency of 430 to 790 Terahertz. Infrared light, on the other hand, has a range of wavelengths from .74 μm to .3 μm and a range of frequencies from 430 down to 1 Terahertz.

While Alex has photographed orbs representing every color of the spectrum, the *Myst* **primarily** presents as white light, with pinks and some blues (discussed in Chapter 2). There are, of course, exceptions. For example, consider the photo below which shows a compilation of three photographs taken in 2012.

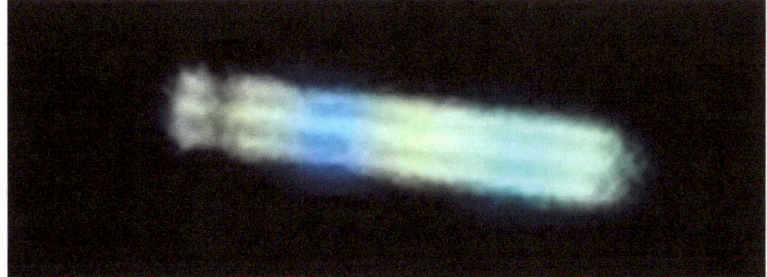

(Above) Unnamed picture (Myst stream) taken in early Summer 2012. The phenomenon was captured in three separate pictures as it faded (same physical location, different placement in the lens).

Looking at the top figure, to the left of this *Myst* "stream" is a face that appears to be reflected in the first burst of light to the right. Can we perceive a continuing line of faces? The three light lines that move through the picture are unusual. The stream moves into a bright blue, a white yellow, and then to a greenish blue. A primary meaning of blue is "truth," although it also denotes "sadness" in various cultures. In contrast, yellow represents "happiness" and warmth. Turquoise is a sacred color in many Native American Tribes. Note that Mountain Quest is situated along a former Cherokee hunting trail, and a number of the *Myst* pictures represent Native American guides or protectors of the land. The range of color no doubt gives us clues as to the frequency at which the light is vibrating. While small Circles can be perceived around the edge of the form, the stream itself is Cloud in nature.

The range of color no doubt gives us clues as to the frequency at which the light is vibrating. When we looked at the stream of angels in Chapter 8, a pattern of pinks (ranging from bluish red to light red) appeared in the *Myst*. Because this color is tied to love, joy and beauty, it is considered higher-order energy.

5. The Myst appears through a "coupling" of molecular physical reality and magnetic resonance physical reality (Tiller).

Enter the possible existence of a second physical reality occupying the same space as the molecular physical reality that we have come to recognize. This second physical reality—based on magnetic resonance—becomes "coupled" to the molecular physical reality through the **power of intent**. The work on intention led by Dr. William Tiller of Stanford University was introduced in Chapter 4 under the subhead "The Power of Intention." The intent expressed by Alex was that of capturing the orbs in her photographs. As she moved through this exercise, and as she perceived response from the orbs, Alex became increasingly excited and joyful, singing and dancing and asking for (and capturing in her photographs) the orbs in different colors and shapes. The first *Myst* forms emerged from this asking, at which time Alex specifically asked the *Myst* to form and shape an animal so that she would have proof of their intelligence and responsiveness. This occurred on October 4, 2010 with her picture of the Llama Pixar. Later Alex asked for responses to her questions and, eventually, she began to direct the appearance of the *Myst* for the purposes of pictures. This appears consistent with the intent of this body of work.

Dr. Tiller's work shows that once a coherent infrastructure has been developed it sustains for a period of time. As Alex went outside night after night asking for pictures, she was building this infrastructure (priming the area); it became easier and easier for her to "call-in" the *Myst*. Further, this is the field of intention to which she invited others to see the *Myst*. During the second winter (2011-12) over 30 people were able to (1) see the *Myst* when Alex captured pictures, (2) capture their own pictures, or (3) be photographed by Alex with the *Myst* near or around them.

(Above) Participants in the 2012 Women of Wisdom retreat held at Mountain Quest Institute calling in the Myst.

Reflecting on the potential connections between Alex's intentions and the *Myst*, it may well be that the human participants who are experiencing the *Myst* phenomenon are acting as co-creators; that through the setting of intent the appearance of forms and shapes in the *Myst* are the result of co-creation.

Chapter 10: Messages from the *Myst*

In our first book, *The Journey into the Myst*, we shared the story of how the phenomenon of the Myst came into our lives and explored the awakenings of early reflections from a Spiritual point of view. Events occurred that we could not understand in any other context. In our third book, *The Heart, the Mind and the Myst*, we will turn our attention to the personal shifts and changes that have occurred—and continue to occur—within the authors as they experience this phenomenon. In this book, the second in the series, we have wherever possible used science to explore the physical phenomenon of the *Myst*, then stepped back to take a more holistic look at what has been occurring.

The combining of science and spirituality is what Freke (2012) calls paralogical thinking. We can have things that appear to be completely opposite yet have a connection, a compatibility, things that are both not logical and not illogical, rather a shifting of perspectives. Taking both approaches together helps us move toward understanding and meaning. We have shared throughout this book—particularly in Chapters 5 through 8 –both our meaning-making processes and our personal perceptions of, and feelings about, the *Myst* forms. In many instances, specific pictures (and the messages they convey) were provided directly in response to questions posed by Alex. While each and every one of these pictures and their messages are spectacular in and of their own right, we now take a systems viewpoint and consider the larger messages from the *Myst*. What have we learned?

Both the orbs and the *Myst* clearly contain information. Recall that information is any non-random pattern, a basic property of the Universe as fundamental as matter and energy.[1] In Chapter 2 we explored non-randomness as probability and provided a specific example dealing with pixel color, followed by an example of non-randomness in terms of response. From these examples and others that emerge throughout the book, we perceive *Myst* as information, **recognizing that information has no meaning until some organism recognizes and interprets the patterns.** It is left up to us to determine the meaning in terms of ourselves personally and the world.

As we unfolded our search for meaning in the *Myst* photographs, we began to notice that some pictures showed similarities to animals and humans that had been a part of our lives. These similarities and repetitive patterns help validate the non-randomness of the *Myst*. Note that the case here is for information, not knowledge. While knowledge always consists of information, knowledge (the capacity—potential or actual—to take effective action) is created within the individual.

Although there are many questions left unanswered, **we have become convinced that there is some form of intelligence behind the orbs and the *Myst*.** Intelligence is defined as the capacity for reasoning and understanding or an aptitude for grasping truths (Websters, 1996). In our theory of the firm based on the Intelligent Complex Adaptive System (ICAS) model (Bennet and Bennet, 2004), we broadened this to consider intelligence as the ability of a person to think, reason, comprehend and act. Karl Wiig (1993) further considers intelligence as the capability to innovate, acquire knowledge, and apply that knowledge to relevant situations. Comprehension is the act of grasping the meaning, nature or importance of something or some situation. **Exhibiting intelligent behavior would then insinuate thinking, reasoning, comprehending and acting with specific relevance to a situation**.

From a scientific viewpoint it appears there is intelligence and thought behind at least some of the *Myst* pictures. There are many patterns that are very similar to ordinary patterns that we frequently use. Examples are animals, human faces, angels, curved beaks and even specific individuals. The probability that those pictures were created by the random appearance of pixel colors is infinitesimally small. And, there are so many of them!

The intelligent behavior involved with the appearance of *Myst* has been observed in a variety of ways. An example is when Alex was asking questions of the *Myst*. She would receive three yes responses (with the *Myst* directly in front of her camera), then would ask the *Myst* to go away for the 4th picture, then ask it to return for the 5th (see Chapter 4). Another example is when Alex asked for specific *Myst* pictures, such as having the *Myst* move through the Corn Maze or asking the *Myst* to pose with the volleyball net.

The question of ***what* intelligence is behind the *Myst*** is much more difficult to discern. In terms of physical reality—and taking into consideration the potential for the coupling of our molecular physical reality with a magnetic resonance physical reality (as proposed by Tiller)—is this intelligence internal to Alex (and others experiencing this phenomenon) or external?

From a simpler perspective, let us consider: Were the patterns created by some external source that is trying to communicate with us? This is a distinct possibility and is strengthened by Alex's questions, her protocol and the results. The sources behind the patterns have demonstrated their intelligence through direct interaction and communication. One example is the two sequential pictures of a Llama that lives in our front field. The first photograph was a normal snapshot of the white Llama Pixar, after which Alex asked (out loud) if the *Myst* would form and shape an animal for her. The next photograph included hundreds of orbs forming a *Myst* Llama above Pixar. This second photograph (which was featured in Volume I of the *Myst* Series) is repeated here.

(Above) The very first "Myst" picture that Alex captured (October 4, 2010). At this point in her experience she was looking at the camera screen, so she did NOT see this with her own eyes. That experience began two days later.

Another possibility is that without knowing it Alex is focusing her mind on some specific intent which in turn becomes reality through the *Myst*. The possibilities for internal influence through the power of intent have been considered throughout this work and, more specifically, in the discussion of Tiller's theory of "coupling" two physical realities, one molecular and one based on magnetic resonance. Since Alex had no preconception of this phenomenon, with no initial expectations, as it unfolded there were many surprises. For this reason combined with what she "feels," Alex is convinced **there is an element of co-creation with this phenomena**, that is, she is resonating (see Chapter 4) with other energies and (through intent) in combination with these other energies participating in some way in shaping and forming the *Myst* figures.

The Dalai Lama suggests that there are three ways that we can understand how things and events come into being. Paraphrasing, these are: (a) the principle of cause and effect; (b) the mutual dependence between parts and wholes; and (c) analyzing any phenomenon, we find that they do not have an independent identity (The Dalai Lama, 1999). Thus, all phenomena have dependent origination and therefore no phenomenon (or thing) exists in and of itself.

Every human being is an intelligent complex adaptive system, and therefore it is difficult even within a single human to trace cause-and-effect relationships. Simultaneously, when we are focusing on a specific part of the system it is difficult to be aware of, and understand, the whole system. While Alex is no exception, we have some level of understanding about her underlying assumptions, values and beliefs as well as her actions and expectations in terms of interacting with the *Myst*. With this baseline, we now try to build some level of understanding about the co-creating force with which she is interacting. For example, what do these patterns say about the intent of the forces creating them? What are the forces that are tied to the physical structure of the patterns?

Could the *Myst* energy be extraterrestrial? While this is a completely open question, our sense is that at the energetic level the separation between the human race and what we call extraterrestrials is a moot point. We presume that the orbs are electromagnetic energy, which is also found in the human form. What is different—as is different within each human—are the *patterns* of the energy. There appear to be many different representations of energy presenting in the *Myst*, that is, energy patterns that may represent different forms of life and potential life, all of which we are just becoming aware.

Can this intelligence be considered spiritual in nature? In a journal paper "The Knowledge and Knowing of Spiritual Learning," spirituality was considered the elevation of the mind as related to intellect and matters of the soul reflected in thought and action (Bennet and Bennet, 2007). The soul represents the animating principle of human life in terms of thought and action, specifically focused on its moral aspects, the emotional part of human nature, and higher development of the mental faculties. There is no question that as the *Myst* started to appear—and as it continues to appear—that Alex is expressing and feeling love and joy, which can certainly be considered an elevation of the mind as related to matters of the soul reflected in thought and action.

Should we be afraid? this is the same question Alex asked when she the first winged figure in the *Myst* with her eyes. The response to her question was her perceiving a hand on her left shoulder and feeling waves of love move through her. In the over two years since that event, Alex has only felt love and joy when experiencing the *Myst*. So, we respond to the question of should we be afraid, absolutely not.

NOW ... By using our imagination and breaking through self-imposed limitations let's see if we can move from information to knowledge.

Masaru Emoto's work (Emoto, 2003 and 2004) with water and Penn State's research (see Chapter 9) have exposed the depth of complexity and power of water in several areas of our lives. Professor Tiller's work at Stanford University on intention has opened our eyes to a potentially strong force of interaction with the molecular reality through focusing our mind with strong intent. Modern physics has demonstrated that "something" can be created from "nothing", and the EPR (Einstein-Poldosky-Rosen) paradox experiment demonstrated that entanglement is real and some physicists believe that information may (in certain circumstances) travel faster than the speed of light. And there are other phenomena in our history that, frankly, make little sense to us. Most of us grew up and live in a world that we perceive as "real" and believing it to be the only one that exists, and it is difficult to accept things that are different from belief systems we have embraced for long periods of time.

Only, nothing is as it seems from our limited frame of experience. This is a lesson we learn again and again in science, and from the perspective of spirituality our world is opening to the fullness of what it can be, and we have the opportunity to do the same. One expression from this viewpoint is "the veil is lifting," that is, we are now able to more easily view energies that have always been present but previously unseen.

These energies have always been around us, an invisible part of our lives and our world. We are not alone. The *Myst* offers the potential to glimpse with our physical eyes the field of continuous energy in which we live. And there is more. **Just as we as humans individuate as we move through life, these energies are individuated.** As demonstrated in the pictures of the forming of the *Myst* (see the Preface), there are potentially millions of individuated subsystems (including orbs and the water molecules that are a part of the *Myst* phenomenon) that coalesce to form larger *Myst* forms. We believe that there may be a point of consciousness within each of these individuated energies.

Everything in the Universe is energy and energy patterns (although there is recently some question by physicists regarding the possibility of information exchange without energy). The orbs and the *Myst* provide a glimpse into the larger field of energy (the Field) of which we are a part. These individuated energies have the ability to act as (and become) one. This interpretation could serve as a model for humanity. One key lesson we can learn from these individuated energies is their amazing capacity to come together in a manner which co-creates larger forms (patterns) that can be more easily viewed by the human observer. Then, when that split second of interaction is over, these energies pull back into their individuated form, a form that is not easily seen by the human eye.

(Above) Individuated energies come together in a manner which co-creates larger patterns visible in the flash of a camera, what we call the Myst.

Can the relationship among the orbs when creating the *Myst* transfer over to the behavior of humans as we move into a higher level of consciousness?[9] Can we tap into the Field to connect with each other, bringing our individuation to bear within a larger whole? We believe the answer is a resounding "Yes." Humanity has already moved in this direction as individuals around the world transverse the Internet and our organizations have become more global. We can't help but reflect on the government directive promoted by the U.S. President in 2008 near the beginning of his first term. This directive called for participation, collaboration and transparency across the U.S. Federal sector. These are the very same elements that shape and form the *Myst*. The orbs energetically participate in the activity of the *Myst* (both as energy and in terms of their excitement), collaborate in creating a larger whole, and become transparent in their creation, melding into form, beauty and presence.

This phenomenon is not exclusive to Mountain Quest. Rather, it is occurring at various spots throughout the world, as evidenced by the increasing number of books on orbs emerging in the market. We believe this is just the beginning of our expanding awareness as a race of who we are and the larger Field of which we are a part. And as in all things, in the course of this book, it is Now for us ...

... the End ...

... the Beginning ...

Endnotes

1: Embracing Stonier's description of information as a basic property of the Universe—as fundamental as matter and energy (Stonier, 1990; Stonier, 1997)—we take information to be the result of organization expressed by any non-random pattern or set of patterns. Data (a form of information) would then be simple patterns, and data and information would both be patterns but they would have no meaning until some organism recognized and interpreted the patterns (Bennet and Bennet, 2008c). Thus, knowledge exists in the human brain in the form of stored or expressed neural patterns that may be activated and reflected upon through conscious thought. This is a high-level description of the creation of knowledge that is consistent with the neural operation of the brain and is applicable in varying degrees to all living organisms. From this process new patterns are created that may represent understanding, meaning and the capacity to anticipate (to various degrees) the results of potential actions. Through this process the mind is continuously growing, restructuring and creating increased organization (information).

2: In the brain thoughts are represented by patterns of neuronal firings, their synaptic connections, and the strengths between the synaptic spaces. For example, a single thought could be represented in the brain by a network of a million neurons, with each neuron connecting to 5,000 other neurons. Incoming external information (new information) is mixed, or semantically complexed, with internal information, creating new neuronal patterns that may represent understanding, meaning, and/or the anticipation of the consequences of actions, in other words, knowledge. The term *associative patterning* describes this continuous process of learning. (Bennet and Bennet, 2009) From the viewpoint of the mind/brain, any knowledge that is being "re-used" is actually being "re-created", and, in an area of continuing interest, most likely complexed over and over again as incoming information is associated with internal information. (Bennet and Bennet, 2008b) See Edelman (2000) for an enlightening discussion on the non-repeatability of memory recall.

Further, when you see a picture only about 20 percent of what you are seeing is represented in the image in your brain; the other 80 percent of that image comes from information, ideas and feelings already in your brain (Marchese, 1998). While this statement may appear a bit strong, the point that is made is that the mind doesn't store memories like a computer, that is, storing everything that comes in. The mind stores the *core* of the picture, what Hawkins calls an invariant (Hawkins, 2004). This particular phenomenon of relating external and internal forms of experience is called appresentation (Marton and Booth, 1997). As Moon explains,

> *Appresentation is the manner in which a part of something that is perceived as an external experience can stimulate a much more complete or richer internal experience of the 'whole' of that thing to be conjured up* (Moon, 2004, p. 23).

For example, if you see your friend from the side or back you can usually recognize who they are since your mind has stored a core basic memory that includes major features of that person. When you see your friend, your mind is filling in the blanks and you recognize the incoming picture as your friend. There is efficiency in this process.

Simultaneously, there is robustness in the way the brain *stores* core memories. If it takes a million neurons to create a specific pattern (the core part of incoming information), the brain may set aside 1.4 million neurons with their connections as space for that pattern, providing a looseness to account for future associative changes (or perhaps for dying cells). Thus, for this particular pattern you could lose tens of thousands of brain cells and still have significant aspects of the core memory available for future retrieval via re-creation. While this may not appear efficient in terms of energy utilization, from an effectiveness viewpoint it is extremely well-designed. Similarly, network theory espouses the development of repetitive nodes built on a distributed information model, thereby creating redundancy. Similar to neuron signals, the flow *among* nodes becomes essential for success. (Bennet and Bennet, 2010b)

3: Dr. Tom McCabe, a mathematician and world-renown cyclomatic complexity pioneer, is a member of the Universal Knowledge Guild. Other members include: Bo Newman (originator of a knowledge calculus and the KFAM knowledge flow modeling methodology), Dr. John Lewis (creator of The Explanation Age model), Dr. Art Murray (founder of Applied Knowledge Sciences) Dr. Francesco Calabrese (the "godfather" of the Institute for Knowledge and Innovation at George Washington University), and the authors.

4: Alex ceased to count the number pictures in early 2012, although she continues to visit and interact with the *Myst*.

5. See The Monroe Institute, www.monroeinstitute.org

6: Dr. William Tiller, Professor Emeritus of Materials Science and Engineering, Stanford University, is the author of *Science and Human Transformation* (Tiller, 2007), a book on esoteric concepts such as subtle energies that work beyond the four fundamental forces which he believes act in concert with human consciousness. He appeared in *What the Bleep Do We Know?* See www.tillerfoundation.com for a complete list of published material and downloadable white papers.

7: Examples of the four types of tacit knowledge (Bennet and Bennet, 2008b):

Embodied tacit knowledge is represented in neuronal patterns stored within the body, and is both kinesthetic and sensory. *Kinesthetic i*s related to the movement of the body and, while important to every individual every single day of our lives, is a primary focus for athletes, artists, dancers, kids and assembly-line workers. A commonly used example is knowledge of riding a bicycle. *Sensory*, by definition, is related to the five human senses through which information enters the body (sight, smell, hearing, touch and taste). An example is the smell of burning metal from your car brakes while driving or the smell of hay in a barn. These smells can convey knowledge of whether the car brakes need replacing (get them checked immediately), or whether the hay is mildewing (dangerous to feed horses, but fine for cows). These responses would be overt, bringing to conscious awareness the need to take effective action and driving that action to occur.

Intuitive tacit knowledge is a form of knowing created within our minds (or hearts or guts) over time through experience, contemplation, and unconscious processing such that it becomes a natural part of our being. Intuitive tacit knowledge may reside in either the potential aspect of taking effective action (knowing how) or the actual aspect of taking effective action (acting). A form of knowing, deep tacit knowledge is created within our minds (or hearts or guts) over time through experience, contemplation, and unconscious processing such that it becomes a natural part of our being—not just something consciously learned, stored, and retrieved (Bennet & Bennet, 2006). In other words, intuitive tacit knowledge is the result of continuous learning through experience.

Affective tacit knowledge is connected to emotions and feelings, with emotions representing the external expression of some feelings. Feelings as a form of knowledge have different characteristics than language or ideas, but they may lead to effective action because they can influence actions by their existence and connections with consciousness. When feelings come into conscious awareness, they can play an informing role in decision-making, providing insights in a non-linguistic manner and thereby influencing decisions and actions. For example, a feeling (such as fear or an upset stomach) may occur every time a particular action is started which could prevent the decision-maker from taking that action.

Spiritual tacit knowledge can be described in terms of knowledge based on matters of the soul. The soul represents the animating principles of human life in terms of thought and action, specifically focused on its moral aspects, the emotional part of human nature, and higher development of the mental faculties (Bennet & Bennet, 2007, 2008c). While there is a "knowing" related to spiritual knowledge similar to intuition, this knowing does not include the experiential base of intuition, and it may or may not have emotional tags. The current state of the evolution of our understanding of spiritual knowledge is such that there are insufficient words to relate its transcendent power, or to define the role it plays in relationship to other tacit knowledge. Nonetheless, this area represents a form of higher guidance with unknown origin. Spiritual tacit knowledge includes the streaming or channeling of information that is outside an individual's personal experience or awareness. An example would be the numerous recorded instances in times of warfare where military personnel under fire have known what actions to take without detailed knowledge of the terrain or enemy troop movement. Another example of spiritual tacit knowledge might be Csikszentmihalyi's concept of flow (Csikszentmihalyi, 1990).

8: The concept of a dualistic world is the tendency of humankind to perceive and understand the world in terms of opposites. This is similar to the opposition and combination of the Universe's two basic principles as Yin and Yang (male and female). In Chinese Taoism, this complementary dualist concepts represents the reciprocal interaction throughout nature, where opposite forces exchange reciprocally to promote stabilization, a concept similar to homeostasis. Within every independent entity lies a part of its opposite.

9: A separate small book of prose (with pictures) by Alex Bennet titled *An Infinite Story* demonstrates this cycle of connection and expression. It is available with soft cover from Amazon.

Appendix A

Textures of the Myst (1)
CIRCLES, CLOUDS and POCKED

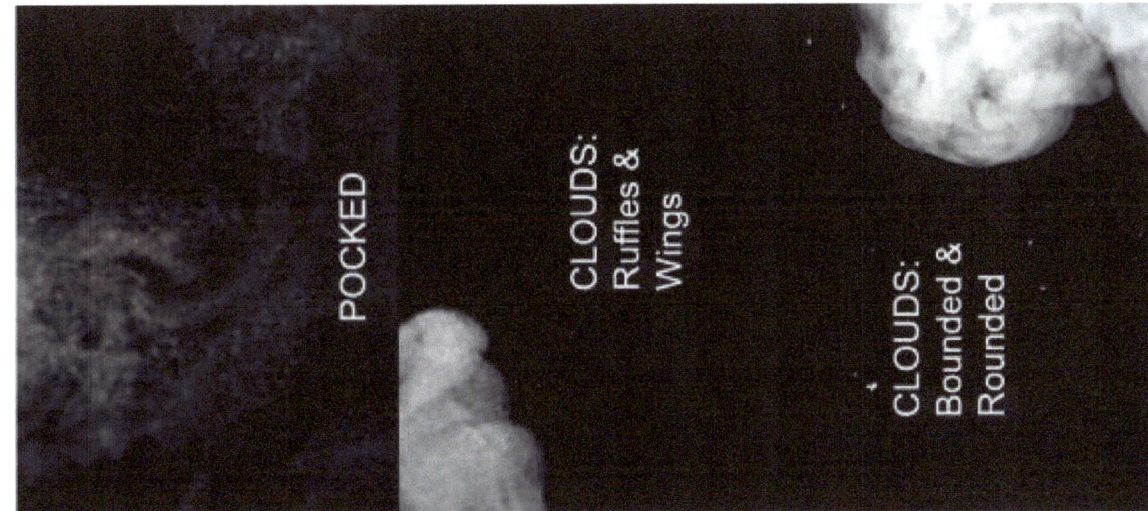

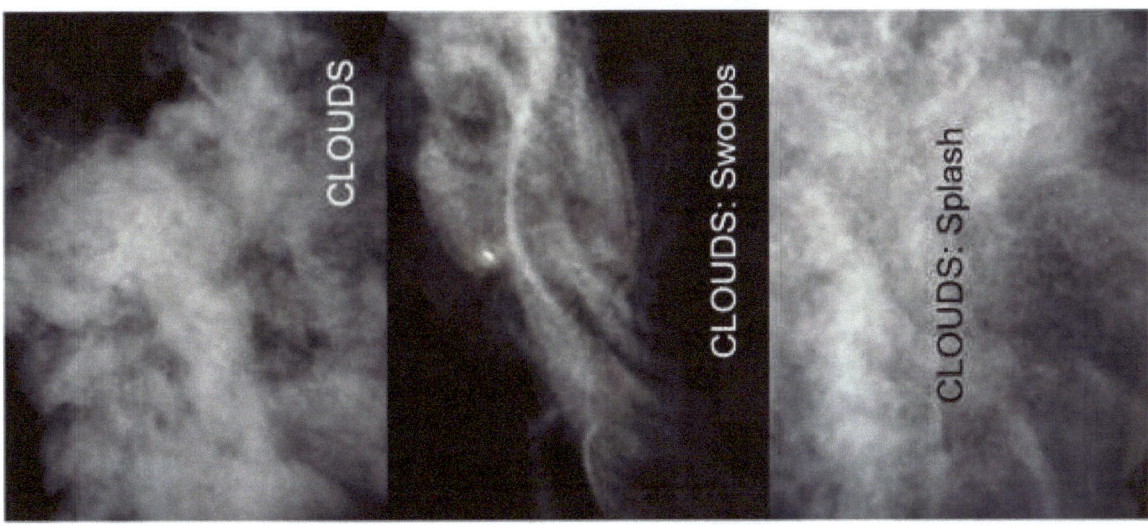

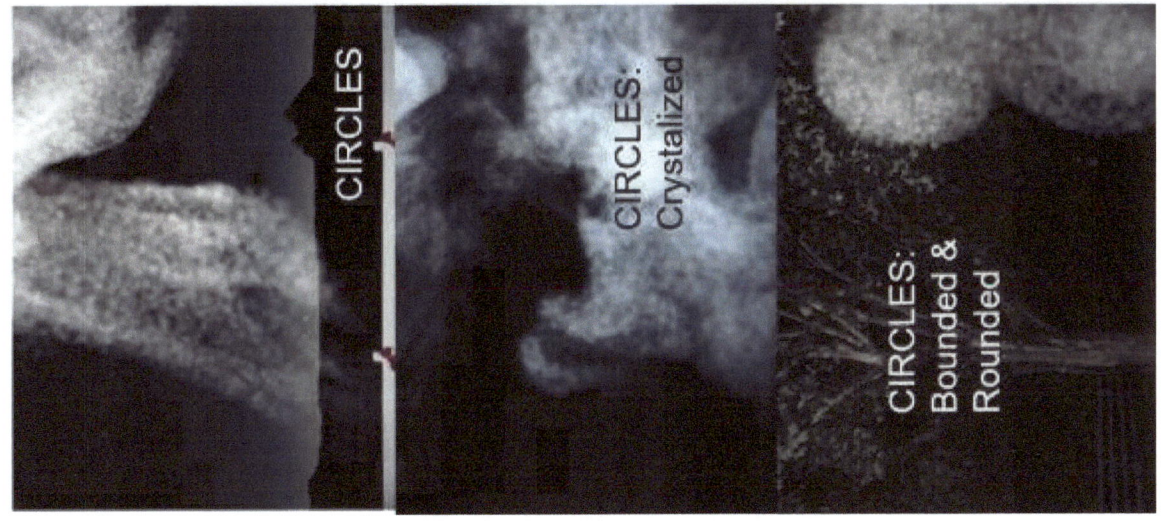

Textures of the Myst (2)

FLUFF, SOFT LIGHT, BRIGHT LIGHT and DOTS

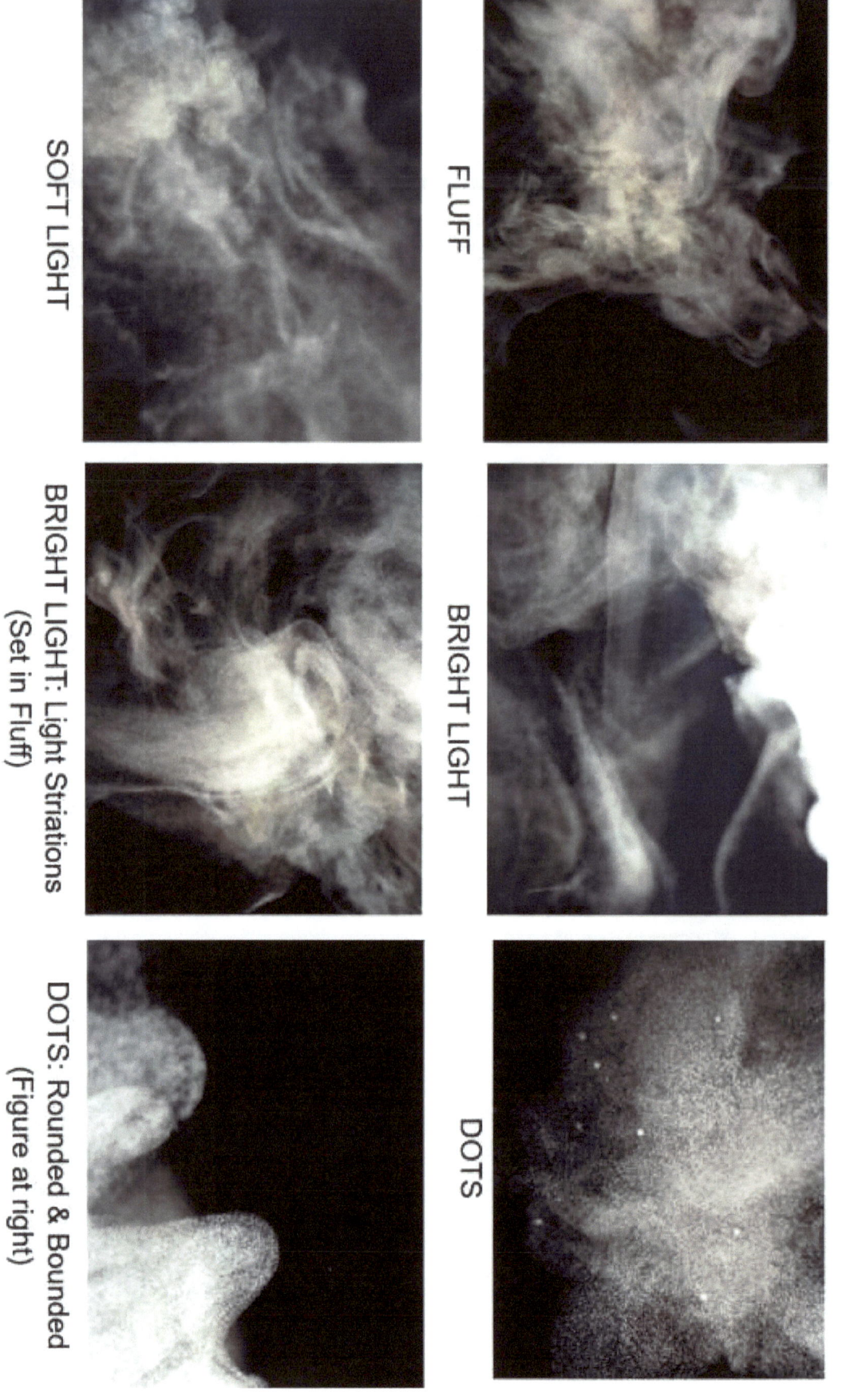

FLUFF

SOFT LIGHT

BRIGHT LIGHT

BRIGHT LIGHT: Light Striations
(Set in Fluff)

DOTS

DOTS: Rounded & Bounded
(Figure at right)

References

Abrams, N.E. and J. R. Primack (2011), *The New Universe and the Human Future: How a Shared Cosmology Could Transform the World*, Yale University Press, New Haven.

Andrews, T. (2005), *Animal Speak: The Spiritual & Magical Powers of Creatures Great & Small*, Llewellyn Publications, St. Paul, Minn.

American Heritage Dictionary (2006), Houghton Mifflin Company, Boston, MA.

Bateson, G. (1979), *Mind and Nature: A Necessary Unity*, Dutton, New York.

Bennet, A. and D. Bennet (2010a), "Multidimensionality: Building the Mind/Brain Infrastructure for the Next Generation Knowledge Worker" in *On the Horizon*, Vol. 18, No. 3, pp. 240-254.

Bennet, A. and D. Bennet (2010b), "Leaders, Decisions, and the Neuro-Knowledge System" in Wallis, S., *Cybernetics and Systems Theory in Management: Tools, Views and Advancements*, Hershey, PA: IGI Global, pp. 21-35.

Bennet, A. and D. Bennet (2008a), "Moving from Knowledge to Wisdom, from Ordinary Consciousness to Extraordinary Consciousness" in *VINE: The Journal of Information and Knowledge Management Systems*, Vol 38, No. 1, pp. 7-15.

Bennet, A. and D. Bennet. (2007), "The Knowledge and Knowing of Spiritual Learning" published in *VINE: The Journal of Information and Knowledge Management Systems*, Vol 37, No 2, pp. 150-168.

Bennet A. and D. Bennet (2006), "Learning as Associative Patterning" in *VINE: The Journal of Information and Knowledge Management Systems*, Vol 36, No. 4, pp. 371-376.

Bennet, A. and D. Bennet (2004), *Organizational Survival in the New World: The Intelligent Complex Adaptive System*, Elsevier, Boston, MA

Bennet, D. and Bennet, A. (2009), "Associative Patterning: The Unconscious Life of an Organization" in Girard, J.P. (Ed.), *Building organizational memories,* IGI Global, Hershey, PA, pp. 201-224.

Bennet D. & Bennet, A. (2008c), "The Depth of KNOWLEDGE: Surface, Shallow and Deep" in *VINE: The Journal of Information and Knowledge Management Systems*, Vol. 38, No. 4 pp. 405-420.

Bennet, D. & Bennet, A. (2008b), "Engaging Tacit Knowledge in Support of Organizational Learning" in *VINE: The Journal of Information and Knowledge Management Systems*, Vol. 38, No. 1., pp. 72-94.

Chambers Dictionary of Science and Technology (1999), Chambers Harrap Publishers Ltd., Edinburgh.

Craig, H. (Ed.) (1951), *The Complete Works of Shakespeare*, Scott, Foresman and Co., Chicago, IL.

Csikszentmihalyi, M. (1990), *Flow: The Psychology of Optimal Experience*, Harper Perennial, New York.

His Holiness The Dalai Lama (1999), *Ethics for the New Millennium*, Penguin Putnam, Inc., New York.

Edelman, G. and G. Tononi (2000), *A Universe of Consciousness: How Matter Becomes Imagination*, Basic books, New York.

Emoto, M. (2004), *The Healing Power of Water*, Hay House, Singapore.

Emoto, M. (2003), The Secret Life of Water, ATRIA books (Simon & Schuster, Inc.), Korea.

Fraser, G (Ed.) (2006), *The New Physics for the Twenty-First Century*, Cambridge University Press, Cambridge, UK.

Freke, T. (2012), *The Mystery Experience: A Revolutionary Approach to Spiritual Awakening*, Watkins Publishing, London.

Hawkins, J. (2004), *ON Intelligence: How a New Understanding of the Brain will Lead to the Creation of Truly Intelligent Machines*, Henry Hold & Company, New York.

Hutchins, R. M. (Ed.) (1952), *Great Books of the Western World*, Vol. 7—"The Dialogues of Plato", *Encyclopaedia Britannica*, Chicago.

Kolb, D. A. (1984), *Experiential Learning: Experience as the Source of Learning and Development*, Prentice-Hall, New Jersey.

Ledwith, M. and K. Heinemann (2007), The Orb Project, ATRIA Books, New York.

Marchese, T.J. (1998), "The New Conversations about Learning: Insights from Neuroscience and Anthropology, Cognitive Science and Workplace Studies" in *New Horizons for Learning*. Retrieved January 19, 2008, from www.newhorizons.org/lifelong/higher_ed/marchese.htm

Moon, J.A. (2004), *A Handbook of Reflective and Experiential Learning: Theory and Practice*. Routledge-Falmer, New York.

Marton F. & Booth, S. (1997), *Learning and Awareness*, Erlbaum, Mahwah, NJ.

Stonier, T. (1997), *Information and Meaning: An Evolutionary Perspective*, Springer, New York.

Stonier, T. (1990), *Information and the Internal Structure of the Universe: An Introduction into Information Physics*, Springer-Verlag, New York.

Mlodinow, L. (2012), *Subliminal: How Your Unconscious Mind Rules Your Behavior*, Pantheon Books, New York.

Pruppacher, H.R. and J.D. Klett (1997), *Microphysics of Clouds and Precipitation* (Second Revised), Kluwer, Atmospheric and Oceanographic Sciences Library, Academic Publishers, The Netherlands.

Soellner, R. (1984), "King Lear and the Magic of the Wheel" in *Shakespeare Quarterly* 35, pp. 274-289.

Stonier, T. (1997), *Information and Meaning: An Evolutionary Perspective*, Springer, New York.

Tiller, W.A. (2007), *Psychoenergetic Science: A Second Copernican-Scale Revolution*, Pavior Publishing, Walnut Creek, CA.

Underwood, S. (Ed.) (2011), *Orbs Around the World: An Anthology*, Xlibris Corporation, USA.

Underwood, S. (2009), *Orbs, Lightwaves, and Cosmic Consciousness: Interacting with Beings from Another Dimension*, Xlibris Corporation, USA.

Virtue, D. (2003), *Archangels & Ascended Masters: Guide to Working and Healing with Divinities and Deities*, Hay House, Carlsbad, CA.

Volk, T. (1995, *Metapatterns Across Space, Time, and Mind*, Columbia University Press, New York.

Wainwright, Stephen A. (1988), *Axis and Circumference: The Cylindrical Shape of Plants and Animals*, Harvard University Press, Cambridge.

Websters Encyclopedic Unabridged Dictionary of the English Language (1996), Portland House, New York.

Wiig, K. (1993), *Knowledge Management Foundations—Thinking about Thinking—How People and Organizations Create, Represent, and Use Knowledge*, Schema Press, Arlington, TX.

Index

angels 36, 39, 56, 70, 71-76, 82, 85
    Mother Teresa as 11, 24, 76
    wrapped in pink 74-76
animals 54-58
    dogs 55-56
    elephant 54
    giraffe 54
    horses 56-58
    jackal 58-59
    predator and prey 59-60
associative patterning 1-2
    brain, in 1, 90-91
boundaries 6, 9, 15-16, 18, 26, 38, 82-83
    borders as 6
classification/clustering system 2
color 2, 23, 26, 42, 79, 85-86
    blue as environmental impact 9
    energy, as 79
    meaning, in 54
    non-randomness of 7-9
    probability of 10
    spectrum of 23, 80-81, 83
energy/energies 1, 17, 18, 23, 24, 26, 51, 59, 70, 71, 80, 81, 82-83, 88-89
    conservation of 4, 26, 45
    electromagnetic 77, 79, 87
    elemental 37-40, 46, 47
    foundational concept of Universe 1
    individuated 88
    juxtaposing positive and negative 58-61
    output, as 2
    properties of *Myst* 82-84
    resonance, as 28-29
    transfer of 4
environment
    external conditions 27-28
    impact on pictures 9-10
    internal conditions 27-28
        see resonance
    weather conditions 80-82
Euclidean geometry 6
faces 10, 40-43
forming of *Myst* 79-80

fractals 6
    Myst as 6
guide clouds 44-45
information 1, 2, 88-89
    (def) 48, 90
    Myst as 49, 85
    orbs as 85
    see patterns
intention 31, 32, 86-87
    power of 29-30, 36, 84
    tacit knowledge and 29-30
interacting with the *Myst* 31-32
    evening of play 32-35
interpretation 1, 48-61
intuition 54
    interpretation, in 1
    knowledge, as part of 48, 77, 92
    listening to 1
knowledge (def) 48
    tacit knowledges 91-92
learning
    experiential 1
meaning 1, 2, 6, 48-61
    approaches to 49-50
    color and 54
    (def) 49
    direction of *Myst* 51-52
    effects as understanding 48
    Dihedral Group Theory 2-3, 49, 91
messages in Myst 85-89
music 69
    and rhythm in the *Myst* 67
Native American 52-53
    shaman 52
orbs 9, 10, 15, 22, 23, 36, 83, 85, 87, 88-89
    intelligence behind 85
    Myst, relationship with 18, 26, 30, 51, 77, 79-80
    responsive 32, 84
    Roy-G-Biv's 23, 80-81
    sphere, as 3-4, 12
    weather, affected by 80-81

pattern recognition
    Dihedral Group theory 2-3
    see meaning
    texture, in terms of 12-26
patterns
    (def) 1
    faces 10, 40-43
    formation 2
    guide clouds 44-45
    information, as 1, 2
    interpretation of 1
    nature, in 2
    non random 1, 6, (def) 7
        response, in terms of 10-11
    pre-existing in brain 1
    repeated 10
    response, of 27-35
    riders of the *Myst* 4647
    shapes as 3-5
physics of the *Myst*,
    energetic properties 82-83
    coupling of molecular and magnetic
        resonance 84
    orbs are integral 79-80
    Tiller, William 91

    water molecules used to form 77-79
    weather conditions affect 80-82
pictures, exploring
    Child of the Universe 64-65
    Cloaked Visitors 65-66
    Crowned with Light 69-70
    What does God look like? 62-64
probability 2
    non-randomness as 7-11
resonance 28-29
riders of the *Myst* 4647
shapes as patterns 3-5
    sheets 4-5
    sphere 3-4
    tubes 5
textures 12-26, (charts) 93-94
    Bright Light 23-25
    Circles 12-13
    Clouds 14-17
    Dots 18
    Fluff 17
    Pocked 14
    Soft Light 23-25
    Squirms 20
water molecules 77-79

About the Mountain Quest Institute

MQI is a research, retreat and learning center dedicated to helping individuals achieve personal and professional growth and organizations create and sustain high performance in a rapidly changing, uncertain, and increasingly complex world. Drs. David and Alex Bennet are co-founders of MQI. They may be contacted at alex@mountainquestinstitute.com

Current research is focused on Human and Organizational Systems, Change, Complexity, Sustainability, Knowledge, Learning, Consciousness, and the nexus of Science and Spirituality. MQI has three questions: The Quest for Knowledge, The Quest for Consciousness, and The Quest for Meaning. **MQI is scientific, humanistic and spiritual and finds no contradiction in this combination**. See www.mountainquestinstitute.com

MQI is the birthplace of Organizational Survival in the New World: The Intelligent Complex Adaptive System (Elsevier, 2004), a new theory of the firm that turns the living system metaphor into a reality for organizations. Based on research in complexity and neuroscience—and incorporating networking theory and knowledge management—this book is filled with new ideas married to practical advice, all embedded within a thorough description of the new organization in terms of structure, culture, strategy, leadership, knowledge workers and integrative competencies.

Mountain Quest Institute, situated four hours from Washington, D.C. in the Monongahela Forest of the Allegheny Mountains, is part of the Mountain Quest complex which includes a Retreat Center, Inn, and the old Farm House, Outbuildings and mountain trails and farmland. See www.moountainquestinn.com The Retreat Center is designed to provide full learning experiences, including hosting training, workshops, retreats and business meetings for professional and executive groups of 25 people or less. The Center includes a 26,000 volume research library, a conference room, community center, computer room, 12 themed bedrooms, a workout and hot tub area, and a four-story tower with a glass ceiling for enjoying the magnificent view of the valley during the day and the stars at night. Situated on a 430 acres farm, there is a labyrinth, creeks, four miles of mountain trails, and horses, Longhorn cattle, Llamas and a myriad of wild neighbors. Other neighbors include the Snowshoe Ski Resort, the National Radio Astronomy Observatory and the CASS Railroad.

About the Authors

Dr. Alex Bennet, a Professor at the Bangkok University Institute for Knowledge and Innovation Management, is internationally recognized as an expert in knowledge management and an agent for organizational change. Prior to founding the Mountain Quest Institute, she served as the Chief Knowledge Officer and Deputy Chief Information Officer for Enterprise Integration for the U.S. Department of the Navy, and was co-chair of the Federal Knowledge Management Working Group. Dr. Bennet is the recipient of the Distinguished and Superior Public Service Awards from the U.S. government for her work in the Federal Sector. She is a Delta Epsilon Sigma and Golden Key National Honor Society graduate with a Ph.D. in Human and Organizational Systems; degrees in Management for Organizational Effectiveness, Human Development, English and Marketing; and certificates in Total Quality Management, System Dynamics and Defense Acquisition Management. Alex believes in the multidimensionality of humanity as we move out of infancy into full consciousness.

Dr. David Bennet's experience spans many years of service in the Military, Civil Service and Private Industry, including fundamental research in underwater acoustics and nuclear physics, frequent design and facilitation of organizational interventions, and serving as technical director of two major DoD Acquisition programs. Prior to founding the Mountain Quest Institute, Dr. Bennet was CEO, then Chairman of the Board and Chief Knowledge Officer of a professional services firm located in Alexandria, Virginia. He is a Phi Beta Kappa, Sigma Pi Sigma, and Suma Cum Laude graduate of the University of Texas, and holds degrees in Mathematics, Physics, Nuclear Physics, Liberal Arts, Human and Organizational Development, and a Ph.D. in Human Development focused on Neuroscience and adult learning. He is currently researching the nexus of Science, the Humanities and Spirituality.

Also available ...

Possibilities that are YOU! by Alex Bennet

This series of short books, which are published under *Conscious Look Books*, are conversational in nature, taking full advantage of your lived experience to share what can sometimes be difficult concepts to grab onto. But **YOU ARE READY!** We live in a world that is tearing itself apart, where people are out of control, rebelling from years of real and perceived abuse and suppression of thought. Yet, this chaos offers us as a humanity the opportunity to make a giant leap forward. ***By opening ourselves to ourselves, we are able to fully explore who we are and who we can become.*** With that exploration comes a glimmer of hope as we begin to reclaim the power of each and every mind developed by the lived human experience!

These books share 22 large concepts from *The Profundity and Bifurcation of Change*. Each book includes seven ideas offered for the student of life experience to help you become the co-creator you are. Available in soft cover from Amazon.

Titles:

All Things in Balance
The Art of Thought Adjusting
Associative Patterning and Attracting
Beyond Action
The Bifurcation
Connections as Patterns
Conscious Compassion
The Creative Leap
The Emerging Self
The Emoting Guidance System
Engaging Forces
The ERC's of Intuition
Grounding
The Humanness of Humility
Intention and Attention
Knowing
Living Virtues for Today
ME as Co-Creator
Seeking Wisdom
Staying on the Path
Transcendent Beauty
Truth in Context

A 23rd little book titled **The Intelligent Social Change Journey** *provides the theoretical foundation for the* **Possibilities that are YOU! series.** Available in soft cover from Amazon

Other Books by these authors from MQI Press

MQIPress is a wholly-owned subsidiary of Mountain Quest Institute, LLC, located at 303 Mountain Quest Lane, Marlinton, West Virginia 24954, USA. (304) 799-7267

The Course of Knowledge: A 21st Century Theory
by Alex Bennet and David Bennet with Joyce Avedisian (2015)

Knowledge is at the core of what it is to be human, the substance which informs our thoughts and determines the course of our actions. Our growing focus on, and understanding of, knowledge and its consequent actions is changing our relationship with the world. Because **knowledge determines the quality of every single decision we make**, it is critical to learn about and understand what knowledge is. **From a 21st century viewpoint,** we explore a theory of knowledge that is both pragmatic and biological. Pragmatic in that it is based on taking effective action, and biological because it is created by humans via patterns of neuronal connections in the mind/brain.

In this book we explore *the course of knowledge*. Just as a winding stream in the bowls of the mountain's curves and dips through ravines and high valleys, so, too, with knowledge. In a continuous journey towards intelligent activity, context-sensitive and situation-dependent knowledge, imperfect and incomplete, experientially engages a changing landscape in a continuous cycle of learning and expanding. *We are in a continuous cycle of knowledge creation such that every moment offers the opportunity for the emergence of new and exciting ideas, all waiting to be put in service to an interconnected world.* Learn more about this **exciting human capacity**! AVAILABLE FROM AMAZON in softback cover and as an eBook.

Expanding the Self: The Intelligent Complex Adaptive Learning System
by David Bennet, Alex Bennet and Robert Turner (2015)

We live in unprecedented times; indeed, turbulent times that can arguably be defined as ushering humanity into a new Golden Age, offering the opportunity to embrace new ways of learning and living in a globally and collaboratively entangled connectedness. In this shifting and dynamic environment, life demands accelerated cycles of learning experiences. Fortunately, we as a humanity have begun to look within ourselves to better understand the way our mind/brain operates, the amazing qualities of the body that power our thoughts and feelings, and the reciprocal loops as those thoughts and feelings change our physical structure. This emerging knowledge begs us to relook and rethink what we know about learning.

This book is a treasure for those interested in how recent findings in neuroscience impact learning. The result of this work is an expanding **experiential learning model called the Intelligent Complex Adaptive Learning System**, adding the **fifth mode of social engagement** to Kolb's concrete experience, reflective observation, abstract conceptualization and active experimentation, with the five modes undergirded by **the power of Self**. A significant conclusion is that should they desire, adults have much more control over their learning than they may realize. AVAILABLE FROM AMAZON in softback cover and as an eBook.

Leading with the Future in Mind: Knowledge and Emergent Leadership
by Alex Bennet and David Bennet with John Lewis (2015)

We exist in a new reality, a global world where the individuated power of the mind/brain offers possibilities beyond our imagination. It is within this framework that thought leading emerges, and when married to our collaborative nature, makes the impossible an everyday occurrence. *Leading with the Future in Mind*, **building on profound insights unleashed by recent findings in neuroscience**, provides a new view that converges leadership, knowledge and learning for individual and organizational advancement.
 This book provides a **research-based *tour de force* for the future of leadership**. Moving from the leadership of the past, for the few at the top, using authority as the explanation, we now find leadership emerging from all levels of the organization, with knowledge as the explanation. The future will be owned by the organizations that can master the relationships between knowledge and leadership. Wrapped in the mantle of collaboration and engaging our full resources—physical, mental, emotional and spiritual—we open the door to possibilities. We are dreaming the future together. AVAILABLE FROM AMAZON in softback cover and as an eBook.

The Profundity and Bifurcation of Change *Part I: Laying the Groundwork*
by Alex Bennet and David Bennet with Arthur Shelley, Theresa Bullard and John Lewis

This book lays the groundwork for the **Intelligent Social Change Journey** (ISCJ), a developmental journey of the body, mind and heart, moving from the heaviness of cause-and-effect linear extrapolations, to the fluidity of co-evolving with our environment, to the lightness of breathing our thought and feelings into reality. Grounded in development of our mental faculties, these are phase changes, each building on and expanding previous learning in our movement toward intelligent activity. As we lay the groundwork, we move through the concepts of change, knowledge, forces, self and consciousness. Then, recognizing that we are holistic beings, we provide a baseline model for individual change from within.

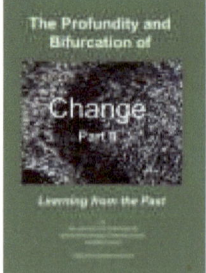

The Profundity and Bifurcation of Change *Part II: Learning from the Past*
by Alex Bennet and David Bennet with Arthur Shelley, Theresa Bullard and John Lewis

Phase 1 of the Intelligent Social Change Journey (ISCJ) is focused on the linear cause-and-effect relationships of logical thinking. Knowledge, situation dependent and context sensitive, is a product of the past. **Phase 1 assumes that for every effect there is an originating cause.** This is where we as a humanity, and as individuals, begin to develop our mental faculties. In this book we explore cause and effect, scan a kaleidoscope of change models, and review the modalities of change. Since change is easier and more fluid when we are grounded, we explore three interpretations of grounding. In preparation for expanding our consciousness, a readiness assessment and sample change agent's strategy are included. (Release 01/15/17)

The Profundity and Bifurcation of Change *Part III: Learning in the Present*
by Alex Bennet and David Bennet with Arthur Shelley, Theresa Bullard and John Lewis

As the world becomes increasingly complex, Phase 2 of the Intelligent Social Change Journey (ISCJ) is focused on **co-evolving with the environment**. This requires a deepening connection to others, moving into empathy. While the NOW is the focus, there is an increasing ability to put together patterns from the past and think conceptually, as well as extrapolate future behaviors. Thus, we look closely at the relationship of time and space, and pattern thinking. We look at the human body as a complex energetic system, exploring the role of emotions as a guidance system, and what happens when we have stuck energy. This book also introduces Knowledge Capacities, different ways of thinking that build capacity for sustainability.

The Profundity and Bifurcation of Change *Part IV: Co-Creating the Future*
by Alex Bennet and David Bennet with Arthur Shelley, Theresa Bullard and John Lewis

As we move into Phase 3 of the Intelligent Social Change Journey (ISCJ), **we fully embrace our role as co-creator**. We recognize the power of thought and the role of attention and intention in our ever-expanding search for a higher level of truth. Whether we choose to engage it or not, we explore mental discipline as a tool toward expanded consciousness. In preparing ourselves for the creative leap, there are ever-deepening connections with others. We now understand that the mental faculties are in service to the intuitional, preparing us to, and expanding our ability to, act in and on the world, living with conscious compassion and tapping into the intuitional at will.

The Profundity and Bifurcation of Change *Part V: Living the Future*
by Alex Bennet and David Bennet with Arthur Shelley, Theresa Bullard, John Lewis and Donna Panucci

We embrace the ancient art and science of Alchemy to **explore the larger shift underway for humanity** and how we can consciously and intentionally speed up evolution to enhance outcomes. In this conversation, we look at balancing and sensing, the harmony of beauty, and virtues for living the future. Conscious compassion, a virtue, is introduced as a state of being connected to morality and good character, inclusive of giving selfless service. We are now ready to refocus our attention on knowledge and consciousness, exploring their new roles in our advancement. And all of this expanding and growth as we move through the ISCJ is giving a wide freedom of choice as we approach the bifurcation. What will we manifest?

REMEMBRANCE: Pathways to Expanded Learning with Music and Metamusic®
by Barbara Bullard and Alex Bennet (2013)

Take **a journey of discovery into the last great frontier—the human mind/brain**, an instrument of amazing flexibility and plasticity. This eBook is written for brain users who are intent on mining more of the golden possibilities that lie inherent in each of our unique brains. Begin by discovering the role positive attitudes play in learning, and the power of self-affirmations and visualizations. Then explore the use of brain wave entrainment mixed with designer music called Metamusic® to achieve enhanced learning states. Join students of all ages who are **creating magical learning outcomes using music and Metamusic.®** AVAILABLE FROM AMAZON in softback cover and as an eBook.

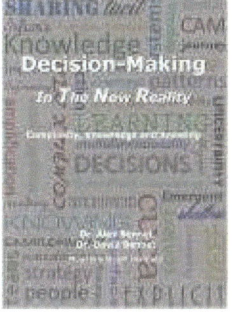

Decision-Making in The New Reality: Complexity, Knowledge and Knowing
by Alex Bennet and David Bennet (2013)

We live in a world that offers many possible futures. The ever-expanding complexity of information and knowledge provide many choices for decision-makers, and we are all making decisions every single day! As the problems and messes of the world become more complex, our decision consequences are more and more difficult to anticipate, and our **decision-making processes must change to keep up with this world complexification**. This book takes a consilience approach to explore decision-making in The New Reality, fully engaging systems and complexity theory, knowledge research, and recent neuroscience findings. It also presents methodologies for decision-makers to tap into their unconscious, accessing tacit knowledge resources and increasingly relying on the sense of knowing that is available to each of us.

Almost every day new energies are erupting around the world: new thoughts, new feelings, new knowing, all contributing to new situations that require new decisions and actions from each and every one of us. A global consciousness is emerging. As complex adaptive systems linked to a flowing fount of knowing, we can each bring these resources to bear to achieve our ever-expanding vision of the future. Are we up to the challenge? AVAILABLE FROM AMAZON in softback cover and as an eBook.

Other Books by these authors

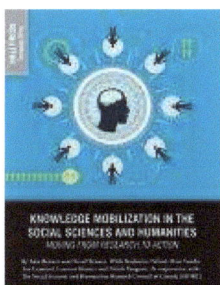

Knowledge Mobilization in the Social Sciences and Humanities: Moving from Research to Action *by Alex Bennet and David Bennet* (2007)

This book takes the reader from the University lab to the playgrounds of communities. It shows how to integrate, move and use knowledge, an action journey within an identified action space that is called knowledge mobilization. Whether knowledge is mobilized through an individual, organization, community or nation, it becomes **a powerful asset** creating a synergy and focus that brings forth the best of action and values. Individuals and teams who can envision, feel, create and apply this power are the true leaders of tomorrow. When we can **mobilize knowledge for the greater good** humanity will have left the information age and entered the age of knowledge, ultimately leading to compassion and—hopefully—wisdom. AVAILABLE FROM AMAZON as an eBook and softback cover (used).

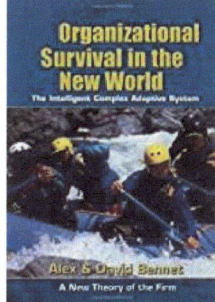

Organizational Survival in the New World: The Intelligent Complex Adaptive System
by Alex Bennet and David Bennet (Elsevier, 2004), available in hard and soft formats from Amazon.

In this book the Bennets propose a new model for organizations that enables them to react more quickly and fluidly to today's fast-changing, dynamic business environment: The Intelligent Complex Adaptive System (ICAS). ICAS is a new organic model of the firm based on recent research in complexity and neuroscience, and incorporating networking theory and knowledge management, turning the living system metaphor into a reality for organizations. This book synthesizes new thinking about organizational structure and provides a **new systems model for the successful organization of the future** designed to help leaders and managers of knowledge organizations succeed in a non-linear, complex, fast-changing and turbulent environment. AVAILABLE FROM AMAZON in hard cover, softback cover and as an eBook.

The Myst Series

(available in softback cover and as eBooks)

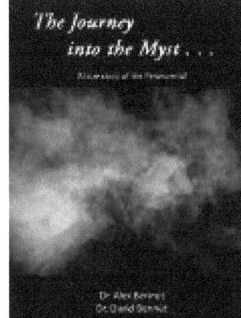

The Journey into the Myst ... A true story of the Paranormal (Volume I)
by Alex Bennet and David Bennet

"What we are about to tell you would have been quite unbelievable to me before this journey began. It is not a story of the reality either of us has known for well over our 60 and 70 years of age, but rather, the reality of dreams and fairytales." This is the true story of a sequence of events that happened at Mountain Quest, situated in a high valley of the Allegheny Mountains of West Virginia. **The story begins with a miracle**, expanding into the capture and cataloging of thousands of pictures of electromagnetic spheres widely known as "orbs." **This joyous experience became an exploration into the unknown** with the emergence of what the author's fondly call the *Myst*, the forming and shaping of non-random patterns such as human faces, angels and animals. As this phenomenon unfolds, you will discover how the Drs. Alex and David Bennet began to observe and interact with the *Myst*. This book shares the beginning of an extraordinary *Journey into the Myst*. AVAILABLE in softcover and as an eBook.

Patterns in the Myst: Messages from the Universe (Volume II)
by Alex Bennet and David Bennet

The Journey into the Myst was just the beginning for Drs. Alex and David Bennet. Volume II of the Myst Series brings Science into the Spiritual experience, bringing to bear what the Bennets have learned through their research and educational experiences in physics, neuroscience, human systems, knowledge management and human development. Embracing the paralogical, **patterns in the *Myst* are observed, felt, interpreted, analyzed and compared** in terms of their physical make-up, non-randomness, intelligent sources and potential implications. Along the way, the Bennets were provided amazing pictures reflecting the forming of the Myst. AVAILABLE in softcover and as an eBook.

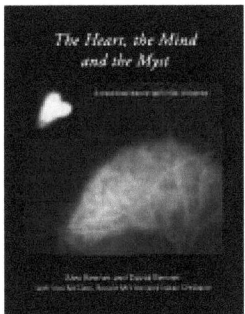

The Heart, the Mind and the Myst: A Neuronal Dance with the Universe (Volume III)
by Alex Bennet and David Bennet with Sara McClain, Ronald McClain and Susan Dreiband

The Bennets shift to introspection in this third volume of the series to explore the continuing impact of the *Myst* experience on the human psyche. Joined by several co-authors, the book unfolds the experiences of a handful of people whose lives have become entangled with the *Myst* phenomenon. So many questions have come to mind over the experiential years in the *Myst*. How does this amazing experience change our beliefs and values? Do we feel and think differently? Do we act differently? What have we learned? And finally, as humanity has entered the shifting times of the 2020's, **how has this experience prepared us for the changes underway today?** AVAILABLE in softcover.

www.ingramcontent.com/pod-product-compliance
Lightning Source LLC
Chambersburg PA
CBHW041959150426
43194CB00002B/60